Power of Influence

Master the Art of Persuasion with Proven Strategies and Techniques to Communicate Effectively, Influence Others, and Achieve Success

Laura Trenaman

Table of Contents

Introduction

In a world where effective communication and persuasion are paramount to success, mastering the art of influence is more crucial than ever. Whether in the workplace, within personal relationships, or in broader social interactions, the ability to persuade others to adopt our ideas, beliefs, or behaviors can open doors, forge alliances, and drive positive change.

Power of Influence is a comprehensive guide designed to empower you with proven strategies and techniques to become a master influencer. Drawing from the fields of psychology, communication studies, and real-world experience, this book provides practical insights and actionable steps to help you harness the power of persuasion in various aspects of your life.

Throughout these pages, we'll explore the psychology behind persuasion, uncovering the principles and cognitive biases that shape human decision-making. From building rapport and trust to tailoring your communication to different audiences, you'll learn how to effectively convey your message and inspire action.

Whether you're seeking to influence colleagues and superiors in the professional realm, navigate personal relationships with grace and tact, or simply enhance your ability to persuade others in everyday interactions, Power of Influence equips you with the tools you need to succeed.

But influence isn't just about getting others to agree with you—it's also about doing so ethically and responsibly. As we delve into the ethical considerations of influence, you'll discover the importance of integrity, transparency, and respect in your persuasive efforts.

Moreover, in today's digital age, the landscape of influence is constantly evolving. From social media platforms to virtual communication channels, the methods by which we exert influence have expanded exponentially. In this book, we'll explore how to navigate this digital terrain effectively and leverage online tools to amplify your persuasive impact.

Whether you're a seasoned leader looking to refine your influence skills or someone embarking on a journey to enhance your communication abilities, Power of Influence offers invaluable insights and practical guidance to help you communicate effectively, influence others, and achieve success.

Welcome to the journey of mastering the art of persuasion. Your path to greater influence starts here.

Chapter 1: Understanding the Dynamics of Influence

In the vast tapestry of human interaction, influence is the invisible force that shapes our decisions, actions, and perceptions. From the subtle sway of a friend's recommendation to the powerful pull of societal norms, understanding the dynamics of influence is essential for navigating the complexities of our social world.

The Power of Influence

Imagine yourself standing at a crossroads, faced with a myriad of choices. What guides your decision-making process? More often than not, it is the influence of those around us. Influence permeates every aspect of our lives, from the products we purchase to the beliefs we hold dear.

At its core, influence is the ability to shape the thoughts, feelings, and behaviors of others. It is a fundamental aspect of human nature, rooted in our innate desire to connect and belong. Whether we realize it or not, we are constantly being influenced by the world around us, and in turn, we exert influence upon others.

The Science of Persuasion

But what exactly is influence, and how does it work? The science of persuasion offers valuable insights into the mechanisms behind this enigmatic force. Researchers have identified several key principles that underlie the art of persuasion, including reciprocity, scarcity, authority, consistency, liking, and consensus.

Reciprocity is the idea that people feel compelled to repay kindness or favors. By offering something of value to others, whether it be a small gesture or a grand gesture, we can subtly influence them to reciprocate in kind.

Scarcity taps into our fear of missing out, making something more desirable simply because it is rare or limited. By emphasizing the scarcity of a product or opportunity, we can create a sense of urgency that motivates others to take action.

Authority involves leveraging the expertise or credibility of a trusted figure to sway opinions or behaviors. People are more likely to follow the lead of someone they perceive as knowledgeable or authoritative in a given domain.

Consistency exploits our desire to maintain congruence between our beliefs and actions. By getting others to commit to small, initial steps, we can gradually nudge them towards larger, more significant changes in behavior.

Liking capitalizes on the power of affinity and rapport. We are more likely to be influenced by people we know, like, and trust, making likability a potent tool in the arsenal of persuasion.

Consensus relies on the principle of social proof, which suggests that people look to others for guidance in uncertain situations. By highlighting the widespread adoption or approval of a particular choice, we can persuade others to follow suit.

The Art of Influence

While the science of persuasion provides a framework for understanding influence, the art of influence lies in its application. Mastering the dynamics of influence requires a delicate balance of empathy, authenticity, and strategic communication.

Empathy allows us to understand the needs, desires, and perspectives of others, enabling us to tailor our influence attempts accordingly. By putting ourselves in the shoes of our audience, we can better anticipate their reactions and adjust our approach as needed.

Authenticity breeds trust and credibility, laying the foundation for genuine connections and lasting influence. People are more likely to be swayed by those who are sincere and transparent in their intentions, rather than those who resort to manipulation or deception.

Strategic communication involves crafting persuasive messages that resonate with our audience and compel them to take action. Whether through compelling storytelling, persuasive rhetoric, or strategic framing, effective communication is key to wielding influence in a meaningful way.

Influence is a potent force that shapes the fabric of our social world. By understanding the underlying principles of persuasion and mastering the art of influence, we can navigate the complexities of human interaction with grace and purpose. As we embark on this journey of discovery, let us remember the words of William Shakespeare: "All the world's a stage, and all the men and women merely players; they have their exits and their entrances, and one man in his time plays many parts." May we play our parts with wisdom, compassion, and integrity, using our influence to uplift and inspire those around us.

1.1 Defining Influence

Before we delve deeper into the intricacies of influence, it's essential to establish a clear understanding of what influence truly entails. At its core, influence can be defined as the capacity or power to affect the thoughts, emotions, decisions, and actions of others. It's the subtle yet significant force that shapes human behavior and shapes the course of our interactions.

Influence operates on multiple levels, ranging from the personal to the societal. On a personal level, it manifests in the form of persuasion, where individuals seek to sway the opinions or actions of others to align with their interests or objectives. This can occur through various means, such as logical reasoning, emotional appeals, or social pressure.

At the societal level, influence takes on a broader scope, encompassing cultural norms, social structures, and institutional dynamics. It shapes our collective beliefs, values, and behaviors, influencing everything from political ideologies to consumer trends.

However, it's important to recognize that influence is not inherently good or bad. Like any tool, its impact depends on how it is wielded. While positive influence can inspire positive change and foster growth, negative influence can lead to manipulation, coercion, or exploitation.

In essence, influence is a fundamental aspect of human interaction, driving our social dynamics and shaping the world we inhabit. By understanding its nuances and mechanisms, we can navigate its complexities with greater insight and awareness.

1.2 Importance of Influence in Various Aspects of Life

Influence permeates every facet of our existence, wielding a profound impact on our thoughts, behaviors, and relationships. From the personal realm of our everyday interactions to the grand stage of global affairs, the power of influence shapes the course of human history and shapes the fabric of society. In this chapter, we will explore the multifaceted importance of influence across a diverse array of domains, ranging from interpersonal relationships to business, politics, and beyond.

Interpersonal Relationships

At the heart of influence lies the intricate dance of interpersonal relationships. From the moment we are born, we are immersed in a web of social connections that shape our identity, beliefs, and behaviors. Influence plays a pivotal role in the dynamics of these relationships, guiding our interactions with family, friends, colleagues, and strangers alike.

In the realm of friendship, influence fosters camaraderie, trust, and mutual support. We are influenced by the values, interests, and personalities of our friends, shaping our own identities in the process. Likewise, we exert influence upon them, sharing experiences, exchanging ideas, and shaping each other's perspectives on the world.

Within the family unit, influence takes on a deeply personal dimension, shaping the bonds between parents and children, siblings, and extended relatives. Parents influence the values, attitudes, and behaviors of their children through guidance, discipline, and example, while children, in turn, influence the family dynamic through their unique personalities and needs.

In romantic relationships, influence plays a central role in fostering intimacy, communication, and mutual understanding. Partners influence each other's emotions, decisions, and actions through gestures of affection, expressions of love, and shared experiences, deepening their connection and strengthening their bond.

Education and Learning

Influence extends its reach into the realm of education, shaping the way we learn, think, and acquire knowledge. Teachers wield influence over their students, imparting wisdom, instilling values, and nurturing intellectual curiosity. Through engaging lessons, inspiring role models, and supportive guidance, educators empower students to reach their full potential and become lifelong learners.

Peers also exert a powerful influence in the educational landscape, shaping students' attitudes, behaviors, and academic performance. Peer pressure can motivate students to excel or lead them astray, highlighting the importance of positive peer influences and supportive social networks in fostering academic success.

Beyond the classroom, influence permeates the realm of lifelong learning, shaping our choices of books, courses, mentors, and learning experiences. Whether through formal education or informal channels, the influence of teachers, mentors, and peers continues to shape our intellectual growth and personal development throughout our lives.

Business and Marketing

Influence lies at the heart of commerce, driving consumer behavior, shaping market trends, and fueling economic growth. In the realm of business and marketing, understanding the dynamics of influence is essential for building brand loyalty, driving sales, and gaining a competitive edge in the marketplace.

Marketing professionals harness the power of influence through persuasive advertising, strategic branding, and targeted messaging, tapping into consumers' desires, aspirations, and emotions to drive purchasing decisions. By leveraging social proof, authority, scarcity, and other principles of persuasion, marketers can sway consumer perceptions and preferences, influencing their buying behavior and shaping market trends.

In the corporate world, influence plays a central role in leadership, management, and organizational culture. Effective leaders inspire and motivate their teams, guiding them toward shared goals and objectives through the power of influence. By fostering a culture of trust, collaboration, and accountability, leaders can harness the collective influence of their employees to drive innovation, productivity, and business success.

Politics and Governance

Influence takes on a grander scale in the realm of politics and governance, shaping the course of nations, shaping public opinion, and shaping the trajectory of history. Political leaders wield influence over their constituents, rallying support for their policies, ideologies, and agendas through persuasive rhetoric, compelling storytelling, and strategic communication.

Political campaigns harness the power of influence through advertising, social media, and grassroots mobilization, seeking to sway voter perceptions and preferences in their favor. By appealing to voters' values, fears, and aspirations, candidates can galvanize support, mobilize volunteers, and secure electoral victories.

Beyond the electoral arena, influence extends into the corridors of power, shaping policy decisions, legislative agendas, and public discourse. Lobbyists, interest groups, and advocacy organizations leverage their influence to advance their interests, shape public policy, and influence the course of governance.

Influence is a pervasive force that shapes every aspect of our lives, from the intimate realm of interpersonal relationships to the global stage of politics and governance. By understanding the multifaceted importance of influence across diverse domains, we can navigate its complexities with greater insight and awareness, harnessing its power to drive positive change and shape a brighter future for ourselves and generations to come.

1.3 Psychological Principles behind Influence

Influence is not merely a matter of chance or coincidence; rather, it is deeply rooted in the intricate workings of the human mind. Behind every persuasive message, compelling argument, or effective marketing campaign lies a rich tapestry of psychological principles that shape our thoughts, emotions, and behaviors. In this chapter, we will explore some of the key psychological principles behind influence, shedding light on the mechanisms that drive our decision-making processes and shape our responses to persuasive messages.

Reciprocity

One of the most potent psychological principles underlying influence is reciprocity. Simply put, people feel a strong inclination to reciprocate kind gestures, favors, or gifts. This innate tendency to repay kindness forms the basis of many social exchanges and interpersonal relationships. When someone does something nice for us, we feel obligated to return the favor, even if it's on a subconscious level.

Reciprocity plays a crucial role in persuasion and influence, as it can be leveraged to elicit favorable responses from others. By offering something of value, whether it's a free sample, a small gift, or a gesture of goodwill, we can trigger a sense of indebtedness in the recipient, increasing the likelihood that they will comply with our requests or reciprocate in kind.

Scarcity

Another powerful psychological principle that drives influence is scarcity. People tend to place a higher value on things that are scarce or limited in availability. When something is perceived as rare or exclusive, it triggers a sense of urgency and desire to obtain it before it's gone.

Marketers often use scarcity to their advantage by emphasizing the limited availability of a product or service. Whether it's a limited-time offer, a limited-edition item, or a limited quantity available, scarcity can create a sense of FOMO (fear of missing out) that motivates people to act quickly and decisively.

Authority

The principle of authority suggests that people are more likely to comply with requests or follow the lead of someone they perceive as an authority figure. This could be due to their expertise, credibility, or perceived position of power. When we believe that someone knows what they're talking about or has our best interests at heart, we're more inclined to trust their judgment and heed their advice.

Authority figures can include experts in a particular field, celebrities, influencers, or even individuals who hold positions of authority within an organization or community. By leveraging the authority of trusted figures, we can enhance the credibility of our messages and increase the likelihood that others will be influenced by them.

Consistency

The principle of consistency suggests that people have a strong desire to maintain consistency between their beliefs, attitudes, and behaviors. Once we've made a public commitment or taken a stand on a particular issue, we feel compelled to uphold that commitment and remain consistent with our previous actions and statements.

This principle can be harnessed to influence behavior by getting people to commit to small, initial steps or statements that align with our desired outcome. Once people have committed, they're more likely to follow through with larger, more significant actions that are consistent with that commitment.

Liking

The principle of liking suggests that people are more likely to be influenced by others whom they know, like, and trust. We're naturally drawn to people who are similar to us, share our interests or values, and make us feel good about ourselves. By building rapport, establishing common ground, and cultivating positive relationships with others, we can increase our influence and persuasion.

Liking can also be influenced by factors such as physical attractiveness, similarity, compliments, and ingratiation. People are more likely to be swayed by those who appeal to their ego, make them feel special, or flatter their ego.

Social Proof

The principle of social proof suggests that people look to others for guidance in uncertain or ambiguous situations. When we're unsure how to behave or what decision to make, we tend to look to the actions and behaviors of others for cues on how to act.

Social proof can be leveraged to influence behavior by highlighting the widespread adoption or approval of a particular choice or action. Whether its customer testimonials, user reviews, celebrity endorsements, or peer recommendations, social proof can provide reassurance and validation that our choices are socially acceptable and desirable.

Understanding the psychological principles behind influence is essential for effectively persuading and influencing others. By leveraging principles such as reciprocity, scarcity, authority, consistency, liking, and social proof, we can craft persuasive messages, influence behavior, and achieve our desired outcomes. Whether in the realm of marketing, politics, or interpersonal relationships, these principles provide valuable insights into the mechanisms that drive human behavior and shape the dynamics of influence.

Chapter 2: The Psychology of Persuasion

In the realm of human interaction, persuasion is a powerful tool that shapes our thoughts, behaviors, and decisions. Whether it's convincing someone to buy a product, support a cause, or adopt a new belief, understanding the psychology of persuasion is essential for effectively influencing others. In this chapter, we will explore the intricate workings of persuasion, shedding light on the psychological principles and techniques that drive its effectiveness.

The Nature of Persuasion

At its core, persuasion is the art of convincing others to adopt a particular belief, attitude, or behavior. It involves the strategic use of communication, influence, and persuasion techniques to sway the opinions and actions of others. Persuasion operates on multiple levels, from the subtle nuances of interpersonal communication to the grandiose stage of mass media and advertising.

Persuasion is not inherently good or bad; its morality depends on the intentions behind it and the outcomes it seeks to achieve. When used ethically and responsibly, persuasion can be a force for positive change, empowering individuals to make informed decisions and take meaningful action. However, when wielded manipulatively or deceitfully, persuasion can lead to coercion, exploitation, and harm.

The Psychology behind Persuasion

At the heart of persuasion lies a complex interplay of psychological factors that influence our receptiveness to persuasive messages. By understanding these psychological principles, we can unravel the mysteries of persuasion and harness its power to effect change.

1. Cognitive Dissonance

Cognitive dissonance is the discomfort we experience when our beliefs, attitudes, or behaviors are inconsistent with one another. When faced with cognitive dissonance, we are motivated to resolve the discrepancy and restore harmony to our mental state. Persuasive messages that challenge our existing beliefs or behaviors can trigger cognitive dissonance, prompting us to reconsider our stance and adopt new attitudes or behaviors that align with the message.

2. Social Proof

Social proof is the tendency to look to others for guidance in uncertain or ambiguous situations. When we're unsure how to behave or what decision to make, we often look to the actions and behaviors of others for cues on how to act. Persuasive messages that highlight the widespread adoption or approval of a particular choice or action can tap into social proof, providing reassurance and validation that our choices are socially acceptable and desirable.

3. Authority

Authority is the tendency to comply with requests or follow the lead of someone we perceive as an authority figure. Authority figures can include experts in a particular field, celebrities, influencers, or individuals who hold positions of authority within an organization or community. Persuasive messages that leverage the authority of trusted figures can enhance the credibility of the message and increase the likelihood of compliance.

4. Reciprocity

Reciprocity is the inclination to repay kindness or favors. When someone does something nice for us, we feel obligated to return the favor, even if it's on a subconscious level. Persuasive messages that offer something of value, whether it's a free sample, a small gift, or a gesture of goodwill, can trigger a sense of indebtedness in the recipient, increasing the likelihood that they will comply with the request or reciprocate in kind.

5. Scarcity

Scarcity is the perception that something is rare or limited in availability. People tend to place a higher value on things that are scarce or exclusive, leading them to desire it more intensely. Persuasive messages that emphasize the limited availability of a product or service can create a sense of urgency and desire to obtain it before it's gone.

6. Consistency

Consistency is the desire to maintain congruence between our beliefs, attitudes, and behaviors. Once we've made a public commitment or taken a stand on a particular issue, we feel compelled to uphold that commitment and remain consistent with our previous actions and statements. Persuasive messages that encourage small, initial commitments or statements can leverage consistency to influence behavior and encourage compliance with larger requests or actions.

Techniques of Persuasion

In addition to understanding the psychological principles behind persuasion, it's essential to be familiar with the techniques and strategies used to wield influence effectively. Some common techniques of persuasion include:

- **Rhetorical Appeals**: Persuasive messages often appeal to logic (logos), emotions (pathos), or credibility (ethos) to sway the audience's opinions or behaviors.
- **Storytelling**: Narrative techniques, such as storytelling, can be highly effective in capturing the audience's attention, evoking empathy, and conveying persuasive messages compellingly and memorably.
- **Social Proof**: Providing evidence of widespread adoption or approval can bolster the persuasiveness of a message and increase the audience's confidence in its validity.

- **Authority**: Citing expert opinions, endorsements from trusted figures, or credentials can enhance the credibility of the message and increase its persuasive impact.
- **Reciprocity**: Offering incentives, freebies, or special deals can trigger a sense of indebtedness in the recipient, increasing the likelihood of compliance with the request or action.
- **Scarcity**: Emphasizing the limited availability or exclusivity of a product or service can create a sense of urgency and desire to obtain it before it's gone.
- **Consistency**: Encouraging small, initial commitments or statements that are consistent with the desired outcome can pave the way for larger compliance with subsequent requests or actions.

The psychology of persuasion is a fascinating and multifaceted subject that encompasses a wide range of psychological principles, techniques, and strategies. By understanding the psychological factors that influence our receptiveness to persuasive messages, we can become more adept at crafting and delivering messages that resonate with our audience and inspire action. Whether in the realm of marketing, politics, or interpersonal relationships, the principles of persuasion offer valuable insights into the art and science of influence.

2.1 Principles of Persuasion

In the intricate dance of human interaction, persuasion is the subtle yet potent force that shapes our beliefs, attitudes, and behaviors. Whether it's convincing someone to buy a product, support a cause, or change their mind on an issue, understanding the principles of persuasion is essential for effectively influencing others. In this chapter, we will explore the foundational principles of persuasion, shedding light on the psychological mechanisms that drive its effectiveness and offering insights into how to wield its power responsibly and ethically.

1. Reciprocity

At the heart of reciprocity lies the age-old principle of "give and take." Simply put, people feel a sense of obligation to reciprocate kind gestures, favors, or gifts. This innate tendency to repay kindness forms the basis of many social exchanges and interpersonal relationships.

In the context of persuasion, reciprocity can be a powerful tool for eliciting compliance with requests or actions. By offering something of value to others, whether it's a small favor, a thoughtful gesture, or a tangible reward, we can trigger a sense of indebtedness in the recipient. This sense of obligation increases the likelihood that they will comply with our request or reciprocate in kind, thus paving the way for persuasion to take root.

2. Scarcity

Scarcity is the perception that something is rare, limited, or exclusive. People tend to place a higher value on scarce things, as they perceive them to be more desirable and sought-after. This phenomenon is driven by the fear of missing out (FOMO) and the desire to obtain something before it's gone.

In the realm of persuasion, scarcity can be a potent motivator for action. By emphasizing the limited availability or exclusivity of a product, service, or opportunity, we can create a sense of urgency and desire in the minds of our audience. This heightened desire increases the perceived value of the offer and motivates people to take immediate action to secure it before it's too late.

3. Authority

Authority is the tendency to comply with requests or follow the lead of someone we perceive as an authority figure. This could be due to their expertise, credibility, or perceived position of power. When we believe that someone knows what they're talking about or has our best interests at heart, we're more inclined to trust their judgment and heed their advice.

In the realm of persuasion, authority can be a persuasive tool for enhancing the credibility and persuasiveness of a message. By citing expert opinions, endorsements from trusted figures, or credentials, we can bolster the legitimacy of our argument and increase the likelihood that others will be influenced by it. Authority figures can include experts in a particular field, celebrities, influencers, or individuals who hold positions of authority within an organization or community.

4. Consistency

Consistency is the desire to maintain congruence between our beliefs, attitudes, and behaviors. Once we've made a public commitment or taken a stand on a particular issue, we feel compelled to uphold that commitment and remain consistent with our previous actions and statements.

In the realm of persuasion, consistency can be harnessed to influence behavior and encourage compliance with requests or actions. By getting people to commit to small, initial steps or statements that align with our desired outcome, we can pave the way for larger compliance with subsequent requests or actions. This principle is based on the idea that people strive to maintain internal and external consistency in their beliefs and behaviors, even if it means adjusting their attitudes or actions to align with their previous commitments.

5. Liking

Liking is the tendency to be influenced by others whom we know, like, and trust. We're naturally drawn to people who are similar to us, share our interests or values, and make us feel good about ourselves. By building rapport, establishing common ground, and cultivating positive relationships with others, we can increase our influence and persuasiveness.

In the realm of persuasion, liking can be a powerful tool for building rapport and gaining the trust and confidence of our audience. By appealing to people's sense of affinity and connection, we can create a favorable impression that increases the likelihood that they will be receptive to our message. Factors such as physical attractiveness, similarity, compliments, and ingratiation can also influence liking and increase our persuasiveness.

6. Social Proof

Social proof is the tendency to look to others for guidance in uncertain or ambiguous situations. When we're unsure how to behave or what decision to make, we often look to the actions and behaviors of others for cues on how to act. This phenomenon is driven by the belief that if others are doing something, it must be the right thing to do.

In the realm of persuasion, social proof can be a persuasive tool for influencing behavior and attitudes. By providing evidence of widespread adoption or approval, we can bolster the persuasiveness of our message and increase the audience's confidence in its validity. This can be achieved through testimonials, user reviews, celebrity endorsements, or peer recommendations, all of which provide reassurance and validation that our choices are socially acceptable and desirable.

The principles of persuasion are deeply rooted in the fundamental workings of the human mind, tapping into our innate desires, motivations, and social instincts. By understanding these principles and how they operate, we can become more adept at crafting persuasive messages, influencing behavior, and achieving our desired outcomes. Whether in the realm of marketing, sales, politics, or interpersonal relationships, the principles of persuasion offer valuable insights into the art and science of influence.

2.2 Cognitive Biases and Their Role in Persuasion

In the realm of persuasion, cognitive biases play a pivotal role in shaping our perceptions, judgments, and decision-making processes. These biases are inherent flaws in our cognitive functioning that lead us to deviate from rationality and make systematic errors in our thinking. While they may seem like quirks of the mind, cognitive biases can have profound implications for how we process information, interpret persuasive messages, and ultimately, make decisions. In this chapter, we will explore some of the most common cognitive biases and their role in persuasion.

Confirmation Bias

Confirmation bias is the tendency to seek out information that confirms our existing beliefs while ignoring or dismissing evidence that contradicts them. This bias stems from our innate desire to protect our ego and maintain a sense of consistency in our beliefs and attitudes.

In the realm of persuasion, confirmation bias can lead us to selectively interpret information in a way that supports our preconceived notions and biases. Marketers and persuaders can exploit this bias by framing their messages in a way that aligns with the audience's existing beliefs and values, thus increasing the likelihood that they will be receptive to the message.

Availability Heuristic

The availability heuristic is the tendency to overestimate the importance or likelihood of events based on their availability in memory. We are more likely to believe that something is true or likely if it comes to mind easily, regardless of its actual probability.

In persuasion, the availability heuristic can influence our perceptions of risk and reward, as well as our judgments of the credibility and reliability of information. Persuaders can exploit this bias by using vivid, emotionally charged imagery or anecdotes to make their message more memorable and salient in the minds of the audience.

Anchoring Bias

Anchoring bias is the tendency to rely too heavily on the first piece of information encountered (the "anchor") when making judgments or decisions. Once an anchor is set, subsequent judgments or decisions are made about this initial point of reference, even if it is arbitrary or irrelevant.

In persuasion, anchoring bias can be used to influence our perceptions of value, price, or quality. By presenting a high initial price or value, persuaders can anchor the audience's expectations, making subsequent offers or comparisons seem more favorable in comparison.

Framing Effect

The framing effect is the tendency for people to react differently to the same information depending on how it is presented or framed. The way information is framed can influence our perceptions, judgments, and decisions, often leading to systematic biases in our thinking.

In persuasion, the framing effect can be used to shape the audience's perceptions and attitudes toward a particular issue or decision. By framing a message in a way that emphasizes certain aspects or consequences, persuaders can sway the audience's opinions and preferences in their favor.

Bandwagon Effect

The bandwagon effect is the tendency for people to adopt certain beliefs or behaviors simply because they perceive them to be popular or widely accepted by others. This phenomenon is driven by our desire to fit in with the group and avoid social rejection or ostracism.

In persuasion, the bandwagon effect can be leveraged to influence the audience's perceptions of social norms and trends. By highlighting the widespread adoption or approval of a particular choice or action, persuaders can create a sense of social pressure and conformity that motivates others to follow suit.

Overcoming Cognitive Biases in Persuasion

While cognitive biases can pose challenges for persuaders, they can also be leveraged to craft more effective and persuasive messages. By understanding the underlying mechanisms of cognitive biases and how they influence our thinking, persuaders can tailor their messages to resonate with the audience's cognitive biases and increase the likelihood of persuasion.

One approach is to use framing and messaging techniques that appeal to the audience's existing beliefs, values, and attitudes, thus minimizing the impact of confirmation bias. Additionally, providing clear, relevant information and presenting it compellingly and memorably can help overcome the availability heuristic and make the message more persuasive.

Moreover, by anchoring the audience's expectations with favorable information, persuaders can leverage anchoring bias to influence perceptions of value and desirability. Finally, by tapping into the bandwagon effect and highlighting the widespread adoption or approval of a particular choice or action, persuaders can create a sense of social proof that motivates others to follow suit.

In conclusion, cognitive biases play a crucial role in shaping our perceptions, judgments, and decisions, particularly in the realm of persuasion. By understanding the underlying mechanisms of cognitive biases and how they influence our thinking, persuaders can craft more effective and persuasive messages that resonate with the audience's cognitive biases and increase the likelihood of persuasion.

2.3 Leveraging Emotional Intelligence in Persuasive Communication

In the realm of persuasive communication, emotional intelligence plays a pivotal role in shaping the effectiveness and impact of our messages. Emotional intelligence, often referred to as EQ, encompasses the ability to recognize, understand, and manage our own emotions, as well as the emotions of others. By leveraging emotional intelligence, persuaders can forge deeper connections with their audience, evoke strong emotional responses, and ultimately, increase the persuasiveness of their communication. In this chapter, we will explore how emotional intelligence can be harnessed to enhance persuasive communication.

Understanding Emotions

The first step in leveraging emotional intelligence in persuasive communication is to develop a deep understanding of emotions and how they influence human behavior. Emotions play a fundamental role in decision-making, motivation, and interpersonal relationships. By recognizing and understanding the emotions underlying our audience's attitudes and behaviors, persuaders can tailor their messages to resonate with their emotional needs and desires.

Building Empathy

Empathy is a key component of emotional intelligence and involves the ability to understand and share the feelings of others. By putting ourselves in the shoes of our audience, we can gain insight into their perspectives, motivations, and concerns. Empathy allows persuaders to connect with their audience on a deeper level, fostering trust, rapport, and understanding.

Eliciting Emotional Responses

Emotions are powerful drivers of behavior, and persuasive communication often relies on evoking strong emotional responses in the audience. By tapping into the audience's emotions, persuaders can capture their attention, engage their interest, and motivate them to take action. Whether through storytelling, imagery, or rhetoric, persuasive messages that evoke emotions such as joy, fear, anger, or compassion can be highly effective in influencing attitudes and behaviors.

Managing Emotions

Emotional intelligence also involves the ability to manage our own emotions effectively, particularly in high-pressure or emotionally charged situations. Persuaders who can remain calm, composed, and empathetic in the face of resistance or conflict are better equipped to navigate challenging conversations and overcome objections. By maintaining emotional control and responding thoughtfully rather than reactively, persuaders can build credibility and trust with their audience.

Adapting to Emotional Cues

Effective persuasive communication requires sensitivity to the emotional cues and signals of our audience. By paying attention to nonverbal cues such as body language, facial expressions, and tone of voice, persuaders can gauge the emotional state of their audience and tailor their message accordingly. Whether adjusting the tone, pacing, or content of their communication, persuaders who are attuned to the emotional needs and preferences of their audience are better positioned to resonate with them on a deeper level.

Creating Emotional Connections

Ultimately, persuasive communication is about forging emotional connections with our audience that inspire trust, loyalty, and action. By authentically expressing our own emotions and values, persuaders can create a sense of resonance and rapport with their audience. By demonstrating empathy, authenticity, and vulnerability, persuaders can build meaningful relationships that transcend transactional interactions and foster long-term engagement and loyalty.

In conclusion, emotional intelligence is a powerful tool for enhancing persuasive communication. By understanding and managing our own emotions, building empathy with our audience, and eliciting strong emotional responses, persuaders can craft messages that resonate deeply with their audience and inspire action. By adapting to emotional cues, managing emotions effectively, and creating authentic emotional connections, persuaders can increase the effectiveness and impact of their communication, ultimately achieving their persuasive goals with greater success.

Chapter 3: Building Rapport and Trust

In the realm of human interaction, rapport and trust are the cornerstones of effective communication, collaboration, and relationship-building. Whether in business, personal relationships, or any other context, the ability to establish rapport and trust with others is essential for fostering connection, mutual understanding, and cooperation. In this chapter, we will explore the importance of building rapport and trust, as well as strategies and techniques for cultivating these vital qualities in our interactions with others.

The Importance of Rapport and Trust

Rapport and trust are essential ingredients for successful relationships and interactions. They create a foundation of mutual respect, understanding, and goodwill, enabling individuals to communicate openly, collaborate effectively, and resolve conflicts constructively. In business, rapport and trust are key drivers of customer loyalty, employee engagement, and organizational success. In personal relationships, they form the basis of intimacy, friendship, and emotional support. Without rapport and trust, relationships can be fraught with misunderstandings, conflicts, and breakdowns in communication.

Understanding Rapport

Rapport is a sense of harmony, connection, and mutual understanding between individuals. It involves establishing a positive emotional bond and a shared sense of rapport and camaraderie. Rapport is built on genuine interest, empathy, and authenticity, as well as mutual respect and appreciation. When individuals have rapport, they feel comfortable, understood, and valued in each other's presence. They are more likely to communicate openly, express their thoughts and feelings honestly, and collaborate effectively towards shared goals.

Cultivating Trust

Trust is the belief in the reliability, integrity, and competence of another person. It involves having confidence in their intentions, abilities, and commitment to act in their best interests. Trust is built on consistency, honesty, and transparency, as well as reliability and dependability. When individuals trust each other, they feel secure, supported, and respected in their interactions. They are more willing to share information, delegate responsibility, and work together towards common objectives.

Strategies for Building Rapport and Trust

- **Active Listening**: Actively listening to others demonstrates respect, empathy, and genuine interest in their perspective. By giving your full attention, maintaining eye contact, and nodding or paraphrasing to show understanding, you can create a sense of rapport and trust.
- **Empathy and Understanding**: Showing empathy and understanding towards others' thoughts, feelings, and experiences helps to build rapport and trust. Acknowledge their emotions, validate their concerns, and demonstrate that you care about their well-being.

- **Authenticity and Transparency**: Being authentic and transparent in your interactions builds trust by demonstrating honesty, integrity, and sincerity. Avoid exaggeration, deception, or manipulation, as these can erode trust and credibility.
- **Consistency and Reliability**: Consistently delivering on your promises and commitments builds trust by demonstrating reliability, dependability, and accountability. Be punctual, follow through on your commitments, and communicate openly about any changes or challenges.
- **Respect and Appreciation**: Showing respect and appreciation towards others' contributions, perspectives, and opinions fosters rapport and trust. Acknowledge their strengths, value their input, and express gratitude for their efforts.
- **Shared Goals and Values**: Identifying and aligning with shared goals and values helps to build rapport and trust by creating a sense of common purpose and alignment. Find common ground, highlight shared interests, and work together towards mutual objectives.
- **Positive Body Language**: Using positive body language, such as smiling, nodding, and mirroring, signals openness, warmth, and receptivity, which helps to build rapport and trust. Avoid negative body language, such as crossing arms or avoiding eye contact, as this can create barriers to connection.
- **Building Rapport Over Time**: Building rapport and trust takes time and effort, so be patient and consistent in your interactions. Invest time in getting to know others, building relationships, and nurturing connections over time.

In conclusion, building rapport and trust is essential for fostering positive relationships, effective communication, and cooperation. By understanding the importance of rapport and trust, as well as strategies and techniques for cultivating these qualities, individuals can enhance their interpersonal skills, build stronger connections, and achieve greater success in both personal and professional endeavors. Whether in business, personal relationships, or any other context, rapport and trust are the bedrock of meaningful and fulfilling interactions.

3.1 Importance of Rapport and Trust in Influence

In the realm of influence, rapport and trust serve as indispensable currencies that grease the wheels of persuasion, negotiation, and collaboration. Without a foundation of rapport and trust, attempts to influence others are likely to fall flat, hindered by skepticism, resistance, and mistrust. In this section, we will delve into the critical role that rapport and trust play in the process of influence, and why they are essential for achieving persuasive outcomes.

Establishing Credibility and Reliability

Rapport and trust are essential for establishing credibility and reliability in the eyes of others. When individuals perceive you as trustworthy and reliable, they are more likely to listen to your ideas, consider your proposals, and ultimately, be influenced by your recommendations. Credibility and reliability are built on a track record of honesty, integrity, and competence, as well as consistency and dependability in your actions and behaviors.

Overcoming Resistance and Skepticism

Influence often requires overcoming resistance and skepticism from others who may be wary of being persuaded. Rapport and trust provide a powerful antidote to resistance and skepticism, as they create a sense of connection, understanding, and goodwill between individuals. When people trust and respect you, they are more open to considering your perspective, exploring new ideas, and ultimately, being swayed by your arguments.

Fostering Collaboration and Cooperation

Rapport and trust are essential for fostering collaboration and cooperation among individuals with divergent interests and perspectives. When there is a foundation of trust and mutual respect, people are more willing to work together towards common goals, share information and resources, and compromise on differences in pursuit of shared objectives. Collaboration and cooperation are facilitated by open communication, empathy, and a willingness to listen and understand others' viewpoints.

Building Loyalty and Commitment

Rapport and trust are key drivers of loyalty and commitment in relationships. When people feel valued, respected, and understood, they are more likely to remain loyal and committed to the influencer, even in the face of challenges or setbacks. Loyalty and commitment are nurtured through ongoing communication, support, and appreciation for others' contributions and efforts.

Enhancing Persuasive Effectiveness

Ultimately, rapport and trust enhance the effectiveness of persuasion by creating an environment conducive to influence. When individuals feel a sense of rapport and trust with the influencer, they are more receptive to their messages, more likely to be persuaded by their arguments, and more willing to take action in alignment with their recommendations. Rapport and trust increase the persuader's credibility, reduce resistance and skepticism, foster collaboration and cooperation, build loyalty and commitment, and ultimately, enhance their persuasive impact.

In conclusion, rapport and trust are indispensable ingredients for successful influence. They establish credibility and reliability, overcome resistance and skepticism, foster collaboration and cooperation, build loyalty and commitment, and enhance persuasive effectiveness. Whether in business, politics, or interpersonal relationships, rapport and trust are the bedrock of effective influence, enabling individuals to achieve their goals, win hearts and minds, and inspire positive change. As influencers, cultivating rapport and trust should be a priority, as they are the keys to unlocking the doors of persuasion and achieving meaningful outcomes.

3.2 Techniques for Building Rapport

Building rapport is an essential skill in fostering connections, understanding, and trust in interpersonal interactions. Whether in professional settings, social situations, or personal relationships, the ability to establish rapport lays the foundation for effective communication, collaboration, and influence. In this section, we will explore a variety of techniques for building rapport that can help individuals cultivate strong, positive relationships with others.

1.   Active Listening

Active listening is one of the most powerful techniques for building rapport. It involves giving the speaker your full attention, maintaining eye contact, and demonstrating genuine interest in what they have to say. Active listening also entails paraphrasing or summarizing the speaker's points to show understanding and empathy. By actively listening to others, you signal respect, validation, and empathy, which helps to establish rapport and trust.

2.   Empathy and Understanding

Empathy is the ability to understand and share the feelings of others. Demonstrating empathy involves acknowledging and validating others' emotions, perspectives, and experiences. By putting yourself in their shoes and seeing the world from their point of view, you can foster a deeper sense of connection and understanding. Empathy builds rapport by creating a safe and supportive environment where individuals feel heard, valued, and respected.

3.   Authenticity and Transparency

Authenticity and transparency are essential for building rapport and trust. Being genuine and honest in your interactions helps to create an atmosphere of authenticity and sincerity. Avoiding pretense, deception, or manipulation allows others to feel comfortable and at ease in your presence. Authenticity builds rapport by fostering openness, honesty, and mutual respect in relationships.

4. Positive Body Language

Positive body language is a nonverbal cue that signals warmth, openness, and receptivity. Smiling, nodding, and maintaining an open posture convey friendliness, interest, and engagement. Mirroring the body language of others can also help to establish rapport by creating a sense of alignment and connection. Positive body language builds rapport by creating a welcoming and inviting atmosphere that encourages trust and openness.

5. Finding Common Ground

Finding common ground with others is a powerful way to build rapport and connection. Look for shared interests, experiences, or values that you can bond over. Sharing personal anecdotes, experiences, or hobbies can help to establish common ground and create a sense of camaraderie. Finding common ground builds rapport by highlighting similarities and fostering a sense of belonging and connection.

6. Asking Open-Ended Questions

Asking open-ended questions is an effective way to encourage dialogue, exploration, and deeper connection. Open-ended questions invite others to share their thoughts, feelings, and experiences in more detail. They demonstrate genuine curiosity and interest in others' perspectives, which helps to foster rapport and trust. Asking open-ended questions builds rapport by encouraging meaningful conversations and demonstrating a willingness to listen and understand.

7.   Using Mirroring and Matching

Mirroring and matching involve subtly mirroring the verbal and nonverbal behavior of others to create a sense of rapport and connection. This technique involves matching the tone, pace, and energy level of the person you are interacting with. Mirroring and matching help to establish rapport by creating a sense of harmony and synchronization between individuals.

8.   Expressing Appreciation and Gratitude

Expressing appreciation and gratitude towards others is a powerful way to build rapport and strengthen relationships. Acknowledging others' contributions, strengths, and efforts helps to foster a sense of recognition and validation. Offering sincere compliments, thank-you notes, or words of encouragement can go a long way in building rapport and trust.

9.   Being Mindful of Cultural Differences

Being mindful of cultural differences is essential for building rapport in diverse settings. Recognize that cultural norms, values, and communication styles may vary across different cultures and contexts. Show respect for cultural differences and be open to learning about others' backgrounds and perspectives. Being culturally sensitive builds rapport by demonstrating respect, inclusivity, and understanding.

10. Building Rapport over Time

Building rapport is a process that takes time and effort. Be patient and consistent in your interactions with others, and invest time in getting to know them on a deeper level. Building rapport over time involves building trust, understanding, and connection through ongoing communication, collaboration, and shared experiences.

In conclusion, building rapport is a fundamental skill for fostering connections, understanding, and trust in relationships. By employing techniques such as active listening, empathy, authenticity, positive body language, finding common ground, asking open-ended questions, mirroring and matching, expressing appreciation, being mindful of cultural differences, and building rapport over time, individuals can cultivate strong, positive relationships with others. Building rapport lays the foundation for effective communication, collaboration, and influence, enabling individuals to achieve their goals and foster meaningful connections with others.

3.3 Strategies to Establish Trustworthiness

Trust is the cornerstone of any successful relationship, whether it's in business, personal, or social contexts. Establishing trustworthiness is essential for building strong, meaningful connections with others and fostering collaboration, cooperation, and mutual respect. In this section, we will explore a variety of strategies to establish trustworthiness and cultivate trust in relationships.

1. Consistency and Reliability

Consistency and reliability are fundamental to establishing trustworthiness. Consistently delivering on your promises, meeting deadlines, and following through on commitments demonstrates reliability and dependability. People are more likely to trust individuals who consistently demonstrate reliability and consistency in their actions and behaviors.

2. Honesty and Integrity

Honesty and integrity are critical components of trustworthiness. Being truthful, transparent, and forthright in your interactions builds trust by demonstrating integrity and sincerity. Avoiding deception, manipulation, or dishonesty fosters trust and credibility in relationships.

3. Transparency and Openness

Transparency and openness are essential for establishing trust in relationships. Being open and transparent about your intentions, motivations, and actions helps to build trust by creating a sense of honesty and authenticity. Share information openly, communicate about challenges or concerns, and be willing to address any issues or conflicts openly and constructively.

4. Competence and Expertise

Competence and expertise are important factors in establishing trustworthiness. Demonstrating knowledge, skills, and expertise in your field or area of expertise builds trust by instilling confidence in your abilities. Continuously developing and honing your skills, staying informed about industry trends and best practices, and delivering high-quality work demonstrates competence and reliability.

5. Accountability and Responsibility

Accountability and responsibility are key aspects of trustworthiness. Taking ownership of your actions, admitting mistakes, and holding yourself accountable for your decisions and behaviors fosters trust and respect in relationships. Be willing to take responsibility for your actions, apologize when necessary, and take steps to rectify any mistakes or shortcomings.

6. Empathy and Understanding

Empathy and understanding are essential for building trust in relationships. Demonstrating empathy, compassion, and understanding towards others' perspectives, feelings, and experiences helps to build trust by creating a sense of connection and mutual respect. Listen actively, show empathy towards others' concerns or challenges, and offer support and assistance when needed.

7.   Consistent Communication

Consistent communication is vital for establishing trust in relationships. Regularly communicating with others, keeping them informed about important developments, and being responsive to their needs and concerns helps to build trust by fostering transparency and openness. Be proactive in initiating communication, keep others updated about progress or changes, and be accessible and responsive to their inquiries or requests.

8.   Demonstrating Respect and Fairness

Respect and fairness are key components of trustworthiness. Treating others with respect, dignity, and fairness builds trust by demonstrating integrity and fairness. Avoiding judgment, bias, or discrimination and treating others with empathy and kindness fosters trust and mutual respect in relationships.

9.   Building Personal Connections

Building personal connections is essential for establishing trust in relationships. Taking the time to get to know others on a personal level, showing genuine interest in their lives, and finding common ground helps to build rapport and trust. Foster personal connections through shared experiences, interests, or values, and invest time in nurturing and maintaining these connections over time.

10. Delivering on Promises

Delivering on promises is crucial for establishing trustworthiness. Fulfilling commitments, meeting expectations, and delivering results build trust by demonstrating reliability and accountability. Be diligent in honoring your commitments, delivering on promises, and exceeding expectations whenever possible to build trust and credibility in relationships.

In conclusion, trustworthiness is essential for building strong, meaningful relationships based on mutual respect, understanding, and cooperation. By employing strategies such as consistency and reliability, honesty and integrity, transparency and openness, competence and expertise, accountability and responsibility, empathy and understanding, consistent communication, demonstrating respect and fairness, building personal connections, and delivering on promises, individuals can establish trust and credibility in their relationships. Building trust lays the foundation for effective communication, collaboration, and mutual support, enabling individuals to foster positive, fulfilling relationships with others.

Chapter 4: Effective Communication Strategies

Effective communication is the lifeblood of successful relationships, both personal and professional. It serves as the conduit through which ideas are shared, understanding is fostered, and connections are forged. In this chapter, we will explore a range of effective communication strategies that can help individuals navigate the complexities of human interaction and achieve their communication goals.

1. Clear and Concise Messaging

Clear and concise messaging is essential for ensuring that your communication is understood by your audience. Avoid jargon, technical language, or unnecessary complexity, and strive to communicate your message in simple, straightforward terms. Use clear and concise language, organize your thoughts logically, and focus on conveying your message with clarity and precision.

2. Active Listening

Active listening is a foundational skill for effective communication. It involves fully engaging with the speaker, paying attention to their words, and seeking to understand their perspective. Practice active listening by maintaining eye contact, nodding or paraphrasing to show understanding, and asking clarifying questions when needed. By demonstrating genuine interest and empathy, you can foster deeper connections and mutual understanding in your interactions.

3. Empathy and Understanding

Empathy and understanding are essential for building rapport and trust in communication. Put yourself in the shoes of the other person, and strive to understand their thoughts, feelings, and experiences. Show empathy by acknowledging their emotions, validating their concerns, and responding with compassion and sensitivity. By demonstrating empathy and understanding, you can create a supportive and respectful environment where open communication can flourish.

4. Tailoring Your Message to Your Audience

Tailoring your message to your audience is key to effective communication. Consider the needs, preferences, and background of your audience, and adapt your message accordingly. Use language and examples that resonate with your audience, and frame your message in a way that is relevant and meaningful to them. By tailoring your message to your audience, you can increase the likelihood that your message will be received and understood as intended.

5. Nonverbal Communication

Nonverbal communication plays a significant role in effective communication. Pay attention to your body language, facial expressions, and tone of voice, as these can convey important cues and signals to your audience. Maintain open body language, make eye contact, and use facial expressions and gestures to enhance your message. By aligning your nonverbal communication with your verbal message, you can reinforce your message and convey sincerity and authenticity.

6.   Constructive Feedback

Providing constructive feedback is an important aspect of effective communication. Offer feedback in a timely, specific, and respectful manner, focusing on behavior rather than personality. Be objective and factual in your feedback, and offer suggestions for improvement or alternative approaches. Receive feedback graciously, and use it as an opportunity for growth and learning. By fostering a culture of constructive feedback, you can promote open communication and continuous improvement within your relationships and organizations.

7.   Clarifying Questions

Asking clarifying questions is a valuable technique for ensuring mutual understanding and clarity in communication. If you are unsure about something or need clarification, don't hesitate to ask questions. Seek to clarify any ambiguous or unclear points, and encourage others to do the same. By asking clarifying questions, you can resolve misunderstandings, address concerns, and ensure that everyone is on the same page.

8.   Flexibility and Adaptability

Flexibility and adaptability are essential for effective communication, particularly in dynamic or uncertain situations. Be willing to adapt your communication style, approach, or message to fit the needs of the situation or the preferences of your audience. Be open to feedback and input from others, and be prepared to adjust your communication accordingly. By demonstrating flexibility and adaptability, you can navigate communication challenges more effectively and achieve better outcomes.

9. Respecting Boundaries

Respecting boundaries is crucial for maintaining healthy and productive communication. Be mindful of others' personal space, privacy, and preferences, and avoid crossing boundaries or overstepping your bounds. Respect confidentiality and discretion when discussing sensitive topics or personal information, and be mindful of cultural or social norms that may impact communication. By respecting boundaries, you can foster trust and respect in your relationships and create a safe and respectful communication environment.

10. Follow-Up and Closure

Follow-up and closure are important steps in effective communication. Follow up on important conversations or decisions to ensure that everyone is on the same page and any action items are addressed. Provide closure by summarizing key points, clarifying the next steps, and expressing appreciation for the conversation. By providing follow-up and closure, you can reinforce understanding and accountability and ensure that communication is productive and meaningful.

In conclusion, effective communication is essential for building relationships, fostering understanding, and achieving shared goals. By employing strategies such as clear and concise messaging, active listening, empathy, and understanding, tailoring your message to your audience, nonverbal communication, constructive feedback, clarifying questions, flexibility and adaptability, respecting boundaries, and follow-up and closure, individuals can enhance their communication skills and achieve better outcomes in their interactions. Effective communication is a skill that can be cultivated and refined over time, and by practicing these strategies, individuals can become more confident, persuasive, and impactful communicators in both their personal and professional lives.

4.1 Enhancing Verbal and Nonverbal Communication Skills

Effective communication relies on a combination of verbal and nonverbal skills to convey messages, build rapport, and foster understanding. In this section, we will explore strategies to enhance both verbal and nonverbal communication skills for more impactful interactions.

Verbal Communication Skills

Verbal communication involves the use of words to convey messages, ideas, and information. Enhancing verbal communication skills can help individuals express themselves more clearly, engage their audience, and facilitate effective dialogue. Here are some strategies to improve verbal communication skills:

- **Clarity and Conciseness**: Use clear and concise language to convey your message effectively. Avoid jargon, technical terms, or unnecessary complexity that may confuse your audience.
- **Active Listening**: Practice active listening by giving your full attention to the speaker, asking clarifying questions, and paraphrasing their points to demonstrate understanding.
- **Empathy and Understanding**: Show empathy and understanding towards others' perspectives, feelings, and experiences. Validate their emotions and respond with compassion and sensitivity.
- **Confidence and Assertiveness**: Speak with confidence and assertiveness to command attention and convey authority. Maintain good posture, speak clearly and audibly, and avoid mumbling or trailing off.
- **Tailoring Your Message**: Tailor your message to your audience's needs, preferences, and background. Use language and examples that resonate with them and frame your message in a way that is relevant and meaningful.

Nonverbal Communication Skills

Nonverbal communication involves the use of body language, facial expressions, gestures, and tone of voice to convey messages and emotions. Enhancing nonverbal communication skills can help individuals convey sincerity, empathy, and authenticity in their interactions. Here are some strategies to improve nonverbal communication skills:

- **Eye Contact**: Maintain appropriate eye contact to convey interest, engagement, and sincerity. Avoid staring or looking away, as this can signal disinterest or discomfort.
- **Facial Expressions**: Use facial expressions to convey emotions and convey sincerity. Smile when appropriate, frown or furrow your brows to show concern or concentration, and match your expressions to the tone of the conversation.
- **Gestures and Body Language**: Use gestures and body language to complement your verbal message and convey enthusiasm, confidence, or empathy. Use open gestures to signal openness and receptivity, and avoid crossing your arms or appearing closed off.
- **Tone of Voice**: Pay attention to your tone of voice to convey emotion and emphasis. Vary your tone to reflect the mood of the conversation, and use intonation and emphasis to highlight important points.
- **Mirroring and Matching**: Mirror and match the body language and tone of voice of the person you are communicating with to build rapport and connection. Subtly mimic their gestures, posture, and speech patterns to create a sense of harmony and understanding.

Practicing and Feedback

Improving verbal and nonverbal communication skills requires practice and feedback. Set aside time to practice your communication skills in various settings and contexts, and solicit feedback from trusted colleagues, friends, or mentors. Pay attention to areas for improvement and continue to refine your skills over time.

Enhancing verbal and nonverbal communication skills is essential for effective communication and meaningful interactions. By practicing strategies such as clarity and conciseness, active listening, empathy and understanding, confidence, and assertiveness, tailoring your message, eye contact, facial expressions, gestures and body language, tone of voice, mirroring and matching, individuals can improve their ability to communicate, build rapport, and foster understanding in their personal and professional relationships.

4.2 Active Listening Techniques

Active listening is a foundational skill for effective communication, enabling individuals to fully understand and engage with others in conversation. By practicing active listening techniques, individuals can foster deeper connections, improve understanding, and build trust in their interactions. In this section, we will explore a variety of active listening techniques to enhance communication effectiveness.

1. **Give Your Full Attention**

Giving your full attention to the speaker is the first step in active listening. Eliminate distractions, such as phones or other devices, and focus your attention entirely on the speaker. Maintain eye contact, nod occasionally, and use verbal cues such as "yes," "I see," or "go on" to show that you are actively engaged in the conversation.

2. **Practice Reflective Listening**

Reflective listening involves paraphrasing or summarizing the speaker's words to demonstrate understanding and empathy. After the speaker has finished speaking, repeat back key points or summarize their message in your own words. This shows the speaker that you are actively listening and understanding their perspective.

3.   Ask Open-Ended Questions

Asking open-ended questions encourages the speaker to elaborate on their thoughts and feelings, fostering deeper conversation and understanding. Avoid yes-or-no questions and instead ask questions that begin with words like "what," "how," or "why." This prompts the speaker to provide more detailed responses and encourages them to share more about their experiences or opinions.

4.   Provide Verbal and Nonverbal Feedback

Providing verbal and nonverbal feedback signals to the speaker that you are actively engaged in the conversation. Use affirmative verbal cues such as "I understand," "That makes sense," or "Tell me more" to encourage the speaker to continue sharing. Additionally, use nonverbal cues such as nodding, smiling, or leaning forward to convey interest and attentiveness.

5.   Practice Empathetic Listening

Empathetic listening involves putting yourself in the speaker's shoes and trying to understand their perspective and emotions. Show empathy by acknowledging the speaker's feelings and validating their experiences.

Avoid interrupting or offering unsolicited advice, and instead focus on listening with empathy and compassion.

6.   Avoid Interrupting

Interrupting the speaker can disrupt the flow of conversation and make them feel unheard or invalidated. Practice patience and refrain from interrupting while the speaker is talking. Instead, wait for natural pauses in the conversation before interjecting or asking clarifying questions.

7.   Pay Attention to Nonverbal Cues

Nonverbal cues, such as body language, facial expressions, and tone of voice, can provide valuable insights into the speaker's emotions and intentions. Pay attention to these cues and use them to guide your understanding of the speaker's message. Adjust your nonverbal behavior to show empathy and understanding.

8.   Validate the Speaker's Feelings

Validating the speaker's feelings demonstrates empathy and understanding, even if you may not agree with their perspective. Acknowledge the speaker's emotions and experiences without judgment or criticism. Use phrases like "I can see why you feel that way" or "That sounds challenging" to validate their feelings and show support.

9. Practice Mindfulness

Practicing mindfulness can help you stay present and focused during conversations, allowing you to fully engage with the speaker. Be mindful of your thoughts, emotions, and reactions as you listen, and avoid getting distracted or preoccupied with other concerns. Stay grounded in the present moment and give the speaker your undivided attention.

10. Summarize and Clarify

Summarizing and clarifying key points throughout the conversation can help ensure mutual understanding and avoid misunderstandings. Periodically summarize the speaker's main points or ask clarifying questions to confirm your understanding. This shows the speaker that you are actively engaged and committed to understanding their message.

Active listening is a vital skill for effective communication, enabling individuals to foster deeper connections, improve understanding, and build trust in their interactions. By practicing techniques such as giving full attention, reflective listening, asking open-ended questions, providing feedback, practicing empathy, avoiding interrupting, paying attention to nonverbal cues, validating feelings, practicing mindfulness, and summarizing and clarifying, individuals can become more skilled active listeners and enhance their communication effectiveness in both personal and professional settings.

4.3 Tailoring Communication to Different Audiences

Effective communication requires the ability to adapt your message to suit the needs, preferences, and backgrounds of different audiences. By tailoring your communication to specific audiences, you can increase understanding, engagement, and receptivity to your message. In this section, we will explore strategies for tailoring communication to different audiences.

1. Understand Your Audience

Before communicating with a particular audience, take the time to understand their characteristics, preferences, and needs. Consider factors such as their age, gender, cultural background, educational level, and professional expertise. Research their interests, concerns, and communication styles to tailor your message effectively.

2. Use Appropriate Language and Tone

Adapt your language and tone to suit the preferences and comprehension level of your audience. Use simple, clear language for audiences with limited expertise or unfamiliar with technical terminology. Adjust your tone to match the context and the relationship with your audience, whether formal or informal, friendly or professional.

3. Provide Relevant Examples and Analogies

Use examples, analogies, and stories that resonate with your audience's experiences and interests. Relatable examples help illustrate complex concepts and make your message more accessible and engaging. Tailor your examples to match the context and background of your audience for maximum impact.

4. Highlight Benefits and Relevance

Focus on the benefits and relevance of your message to your audience's interests, needs, and concerns. Emphasize how your message relates to their goals, challenges, or aspirations, and highlight the value it offers them personally. Tailor your message to address their specific concerns and motivations for better engagement and buy-in.

5. Adjust Communication Channels

Consider the preferred communication channels of your audience and tailor your message accordingly. Some audiences may prefer face-to-face meetings, while others may prefer email, phone calls, or social media. Use the channels that are most accessible and convenient for your audience to ensure your message reaches them effectively.

6.   Adapt to Cultural Differences

Be mindful of cultural differences and norms when communicating with diverse audiences. Respect cultural sensitivities, customs, and communication styles to avoid misunderstandings or offense. Adapt your message and approach to align with the cultural expectations of your audience for better rapport and understanding.

7.   Customize Content Delivery

Customize the delivery of your message to suit the preferences and learning styles of your audience. Some audiences may prefer visual aids, such as slides or infographics, while others may prefer verbal explanations or hands-on demonstrations. Tailor your content delivery to accommodate different learning preferences and enhance comprehension.

8.   Address Specific Concerns

Anticipate and address specific concerns or objections that your audience may have. Tailor your message to alleviate their concerns, provide reassurance, or offer solutions to their challenges. Acknowledge their perspectives and address any potential barriers to acceptance or buy-in for more effective communication.

9. Seek Feedback and Adapt

Seek feedback from your audience to gauge their understanding, engagement, and receptivity to your message. Listen to their feedback and adjust your communication approach accordingly. Continuously adapt and refine your message based on audience feedback to ensure its effectiveness and relevance.

10. Be Authentic and Genuine

Above all, be authentic and genuine in your communication with different audiences. Show sincerity, empathy, and respect for your audience's perspectives and experiences. Build trust and rapport by being transparent, honest, and true to yourself in your interactions.

Tailoring communication to different audiences is essential for effective communication and meaningful connections. By understanding your audience, using appropriate language and tone, providing relevant examples and analogies, highlighting benefits and relevance, adjusting communication channels, adapting to cultural differences, customizing content delivery, addressing specific concerns, seeking feedback, and being authentic and genuine, individuals can enhance their communication effectiveness and build stronger relationships with diverse audiences. Tailored communication fosters understanding, engagement, and receptivity, leading to better outcomes and mutual respect in personal and professional interactions.

Chapter 5: Understanding Your Audience

Understanding your audience is paramount to effective communication and successful outcomes in any endeavor. In this chapter, we delve into the importance of comprehending the needs, preferences, and characteristics of your audience. By gaining insight into who they are, what they value, and how they perceive information, you can tailor your message to resonate deeply and achieve your communication objectives.

1.　Importance of Audience Understanding

Understanding your audience is the cornerstone of effective communication. It enables you to craft messages that are relevant, engaging, and persuasive. By knowing your audience's demographics, interests, and motivations, you can tailor your communication to resonate with their needs and preferences. This enhances the likelihood of your message being received positively and acted upon.

2.　Demographic Analysis

Demographic analysis involves gathering data on your audience's age, gender, education level, income, occupation, and other relevant factors. Understanding these demographics provides valuable insights into your audience's characteristics and helps you segment them into distinct groups with unique communication needs.

3.   Psychographic Understanding

Psychographic understanding delves deeper into your audience's beliefs, values, attitudes, and lifestyles. It explores their interests, hobbies, preferences, and aspirations, offering a more nuanced understanding of their motivations and behaviors. Psychographic insights enable you to tailor your message to resonate with your audience's values and interests.

4.   Communication Preferences

Understanding your audience's communication preferences is crucial for delivering your message through the most effective channels. Some audiences may prefer face-to-face interactions, while others may prefer digital communication or written materials. By aligning your communication channels with your audience's preferences, you can maximize engagement and receptivity.

5.   Information Processing Styles

People process information differently based on their cognitive styles and preferences. Some may prefer detailed, analytical information, while others may respond better to visual aids or storytelling. Understanding your audience's information processing styles enables you to present information in a format that maximizes comprehension and retention.

6. Cultural Sensitivity

Cultural sensitivity is essential when communicating with diverse audiences. Cultural norms, values, and communication styles vary across different groups, and it's essential to respect and adapt to these differences. Being culturally sensitive ensures that your message is received positively and avoids misunderstandings or offense.

7. Feedback Mechanisms

Establishing feedback mechanisms allows you to continuously monitor and assess your audience's response to your communication efforts. Solicit feedback through surveys, interviews, or focus groups to gauge your audience's understanding, engagement, and satisfaction. Use this feedback to refine and improve your communication strategies over time.

8. Empathy and Perspective-Taking

Empathy and perspective-taking are critical skills for understanding your audience on a deeper level. Put yourself in your audience's shoes and consider their perspectives, needs, and concerns. Empathizing with your audience enables you to tailor your message to address their specific challenges and motivations more effectively.

9. Flexibility and Adaptability

Flexibility and adaptability are essential when communicating with diverse audiences. Be prepared to adjust your message, tone, and delivery based on your audience's feedback and reactions. Being flexible allows you to meet your audience where they are and ensure that your message resonates with their unique needs and preferences.

10. Continuous Learning and Improvement

Understanding your audience is an ongoing process that requires continuous learning and improvement. Stay attuned to changes in your audience's demographics, preferences, and behaviors, and adjust your communication strategies accordingly. By continuously refining your understanding of your audience, you can ensure that your communication efforts remain relevant and effective.

Understanding your audience is fundamental to effective communication and successful outcomes. By gaining insights into your audience's demographics, psychographics, communication preferences, information processing styles, cultural sensitivities, and feedback mechanisms, you can tailor your message to resonate deeply and achieve your communication objectives. Empathy, flexibility, and continuous learning are key to building strong connections with your audience and delivering messages that inspire, inform, and engage. By prioritizing audience understanding in your communication efforts, you can enhance your effectiveness as a communicator and achieve greater impact in your personal and professional interactions.

5.1 Identifying Different Personality Types

Understanding different personality types is crucial for effective communication and relationship-building. By recognizing the traits, preferences, and tendencies associated with various personality types, you can adapt your communication style to better connect with individuals and foster positive interactions. In this section, we will explore common personality types and strategies for identifying and engaging with each one.

1. The Analytical Thinker

Analytical thinkers are logical, detail-oriented individuals who thrive on facts, data, and rational arguments. They prefer structured, organized communication and value precision and accuracy. To identify an analytical thinker, look for traits such as a preference for systematic approaches, attention to detail, and a tendency to analyze information thoroughly.

2. The Creative Innovator

Creative innovators are imaginative, visionary individuals who excel at generating new ideas and solutions. They thrive on inspiration, experimentation, and thinking outside the box. To identify a creative innovator, look for traits such as curiosity, openness to new experiences, and a penchant for unconventional thinking and problem-solving.

3.   The Social Connector

Social connectors are outgoing, charismatic individuals who excel at building relationships and fostering connections. They thrive on social interaction, collaboration, and teamwork. To identify a social connector, look for traits such as friendliness, empathy, and a natural ability to engage and influence others.

4.   The Practical Realist

Practical realists are grounded, pragmatic individuals who prioritize practicality, efficiency, and tangible results. They prefer straightforward, no-nonsense communication and value realism and pragmatism. To identify a practical realist, look for traits such as a focus on concrete outcomes, a preference for simplicity, and a practical approach to problem-solving.

5.   The Empathetic Supporter

Empathetic supporters are compassionate, nurturing individuals who excel at providing emotional support and guidance. They thrive on empathy, understanding, and helping others. To identify an empathetic supporter, look for traits such as sensitivity to others' feelings, a willingness to listen and offer support, and a nurturing demeanor.

6.   The Assertive Leader

Assertive leaders are confident, decisive individuals who excel at taking charge and leading others. They thrive on challenge, responsibility, and achieving goals. To identify an assertive leader, look for traits such as confidence, assertiveness, and a natural ability to inspire and motivate others.

7.   The Diplomatic Mediator

Diplomatic mediators are diplomatic, tactful individuals who excel at resolving conflicts and facilitating compromise. They thrive on harmony, consensus-building, and finding common ground. To identify a diplomatic mediator, look for traits such as diplomacy, tactfulness, and a knack for navigating sensitive situations with grace and poise.

8.   The Curious Learner

Curious learners are inquisitive, intellectually curious individuals who excel at seeking out knowledge and understanding. They thrive on exploration, discovery, and lifelong learning. To identify a curious learner, look for traits such as a thirst for knowledge, curiosity about the world, and a passion for learning new things.

9. The Organized Planner

Organized planners are methodical, disciplined individuals who excel at planning, organizing, and executing tasks efficiently. They thrive on structure, order, and predictability. To identify an organized planner, look for traits such as meticulousness, attention to detail, and a preference for well-defined processes and routines.

10. The Spontaneous Adventurer

Spontaneous adventurers are free-spirited, spontaneous individuals who excel at embracing uncertainty and spontaneity. They thrive on excitement, novelty, and living in the moment. To identify a spontaneous adventurer, look for traits such as spontaneity, enthusiasm, and a willingness to take risks and embrace new experiences.

Identifying different personality types enables you to tailor your communication approach to better connect with individuals and build rapport. By recognizing the traits, preferences, and tendencies associated with each personality type, you can adapt your communication style to resonate with their unique needs and preferences. Whether you're engaging with analytical thinkers, creative innovators, social connectors, practical realists, empathetic supporters, assertive leaders, diplomatic mediators, curious learners, organized planners, or spontaneous adventurers, understanding their personality type empowers you to communicate more effectively and foster positive relationships.

5.2 Adapting Influence Strategies to Suit Different Personalities

Influence strategies are powerful tools for persuading and motivating others, but their effectiveness can vary depending on the personality type of the individual you're trying to influence. By adapting your influence strategies to suit different personalities, you can increase your chances of success and build stronger connections with others. In this section, we will explore how to tailor influence strategies to different personality types.

1. **For Analytical Thinkers**

Analytical thinkers value logic, reason, and evidence-based arguments. When influencing an analytical thinker, focus on providing factual information, logical reasoning, and data-driven evidence to support your points. Present your arguments in a structured, organized manner, and be prepared to answer detailed questions and address any concerns they may have.

2. **For Creative Innovators**

Creative innovators thrive on inspiration, novelty, and unconventional ideas. To influence a creative innovator, appeal to their imagination and creativity. Present your ideas creatively and engagingly, using visual aids, storytelling, and brainstorming techniques to stimulate their creativity and spark their interest.

3.   For Social Connectors

Social connectors value relationships, collaboration, and social interaction. When influencing a social connector, focus on building rapport, establishing trust, and appealing to their emotions. Emphasize the social impact of your ideas, highlight how they can benefit others, and involve them in collaborative decision-making processes to leverage their influence within their social networks.

4.   For Practical Realists

Practical realists prioritize practicality, efficiency, and tangible results. When influencing a practical realist, focus on presenting clear, actionable solutions that address their practical concerns and goals. Highlight the immediate benefits and real-world applications of your ideas, and provide concrete examples or case studies to demonstrate their effectiveness in practical terms.

5.   For Empathetic Supporters

Empathetic supporters value compassion, empathy, and emotional connection. To influence an empathetic supporter, appeal to their emotions and demonstrate empathy for their concerns and perspectives. Share personal stories or testimonials that evoke empathy highlight the human impact of your ideas, and emphasize how they align with their values and beliefs.

6.   For Assertive Leaders

Assertive leaders value confidence, decisiveness, and achievement. When influencing an assertive leader, focus on presenting bold, ambitious ideas that align with their vision and goals. Demonstrate confidence in your ideas and abilities, and appeal to their desire for leadership and success. Frame your arguments in terms of opportunities for growth, innovation, and leadership.

7.   For Diplomatic Mediators

Diplomatic mediators value harmony, consensus-building, and conflict resolution. To influence a diplomatic mediator, focus on fostering cooperation, compromise, and mutual understanding. Highlight areas of common ground and shared interests, and present your ideas as win-win solutions that benefit all parties involved. Be diplomatic and tactful in your approach, and avoid confrontation or conflict.

8.   For Curious Learners

Curious learners value knowledge, exploration, and intellectual stimulation. When influencing a curious learner, focus on providing opportunities for learning, discovery, and personal growth. Present your ideas as opportunities for exploration and intellectual engagement, and encourage them to ask questions and seek out additional information. Share resources, articles, or research findings that pique their curiosity and stimulate their intellect.

9.   For Organized Planners

Organized planners value structure, efficiency, and predictability. To influence an organized planner, focus on presenting well-organized, detailed plans and strategies that align with their goals and priorities. Provide clear timelines, milestones, and action steps, and emphasize how your ideas fit into their existing plans and workflows. Be respectful of their need for order and predictability, and avoid introducing unnecessary complexity or uncertainty.

10. For Spontaneous Adventurers

Spontaneous adventurers value spontaneity, excitement, and new experiences. When influencing a spontaneous adventurer, focus on highlighting the novelty, excitement, and adventure inherent in your ideas. Present your ideas as opportunities for fun, exploration, and adventure, and appeal to their sense of curiosity and spontaneity. Be flexible and adaptable in your approach, and embrace opportunities for creativity and experimentation.

By understanding the preferences, motivations, and communication styles of different personality types, you can tailor your approach to resonate with their unique needs and preferences. Whether you're influencing analytical thinkers, creative innovators, social connectors, practical realists, empathetic supporters, assertive leaders, diplomatic mediators, curious learners, organized planners, or spontaneous adventurers, adapting your influence strategies enables you to build stronger connections, foster positive relationships, and achieve your communication objectives with greater success.

5.3 Crafting Messages that Resonate

Crafting messages that resonate with your audience is essential for effective communication and influence. By understanding your audience's needs, preferences, and values, you can tailor your messages to capture their attention, evoke emotion, and inspire action. In this section, we will explore strategies for crafting messages that resonate with different audiences.

1. Know Your Audience

Before crafting your message, take the time to understand your audience's demographics, psychographics, and communication preferences. Consider factors such as their age, gender, interests, values, and preferred communication channels. Tailoring your message to align with your audience's preferences increases its relevance and resonance.

2. Identify Key Pain Points and Desires

Identify the key pain points, challenges, and desires of your audience. What problems are they facing, and what solutions are they seeking? By addressing their most pressing concerns and aspirations, you can create messages that resonate deeply and capture their attention.

3. Use Emotional Appeal

Emotions play a powerful role in shaping human behavior and decision-making. Incorporate emotional appeal into your messages by tapping into your audience's emotions, such as joy, fear, hope, or empathy. Use storytelling, vivid imagery, and evocative language to evoke emotion and create a strong emotional connection with your audience.

4. Highlight Benefits and Solutions

Focus on highlighting the benefits and solutions that your message offers to your audience. Communicate how your message addresses their needs, solves their problems, or fulfills their desires. Emphasize the positive outcomes and tangible benefits of taking action on your message to motivate your audience to engage and respond.

5. Keep it Simple and Clear

Simplicity and clarity are key to crafting messages that resonate with your audience. Avoid jargon, technical language, or unnecessary complexity that may confuse or overwhelm your audience. Use simple, straightforward language and clear messaging to ensure that your audience understands and retains your message.

6. Use Social Proof and Authority

Utilize social proof and authority to enhance the credibility and persuasiveness of your message. Incorporate testimonials, endorsements, or case studies that demonstrate how others have benefited from your message. Highlight your expertise, credentials, or achievements to establish credibility and authority in your field.

7. Create a Call to Action

Include a clear and compelling call to action in your message to prompt your audience to take the desired action. Whether it's making a purchase, signing up for a newsletter, or participating in an event, clearly communicate what you want your audience to do next. Use action-oriented language and urgency to motivate immediate response.

8. Personalize Your Message

Personalization enhances the relevance and resonance of your message by addressing your audience's individual needs and preferences. Use personalized salutations, references to past interactions, or customized content based on your audience's interests or behavior. Tailoring your message to each individual strengthens the connection and engagement with your audience.

9. Test and Iterate

Test different messaging strategies and monitor their effectiveness in resonating with your audience. Use A/B testing, surveys, or feedback mechanisms to gather data on how your audience responds to different messages. Iterate and refine your messaging based on the insights gained to continuously improve its resonance and impact.

10. Be Authentic and Genuine

Authenticity and genuineness are essential for crafting messages that resonate with your audience. Stay true to your values, beliefs, and brand identity in your messaging, and avoid using manipulative or deceptive tactics. Build trust and credibility with your audience by being transparent, honest, and authentic in your communication.

Crafting messages that resonate with your audience requires a deep understanding of their needs, preferences, and values. By knowing your audience, identifying key pain points and desires, using emotional appeal, highlighting benefits and solutions, keeping your message simple and clear, leveraging social proof and authority, creating a clear call to action, personalizing your message, testing, and iterating, and being authentic and genuine, you can create messages that capture attention, evoke emotion, and inspire action. Effective message crafting strengthens the connection and engagement with your audience, leading to greater influence and impact in your communication efforts.

Chapter 6: Influence in Professional Settings

Influence plays a pivotal role in professional settings, shaping interactions, decisions, and outcomes in the workplace. Understanding how to wield influence effectively can empower individuals to achieve their goals, build strong relationships, and drive success in their careers. In this chapter, we will explore the dynamics of influence in professional settings and strategies for harnessing its power.

1. The Importance of Influence in the Workplace

Influence is a critical skill for navigating the complex dynamics of the workplace. Whether you're leading a team, collaborating with colleagues, or negotiating with stakeholders, your ability to influence others can determine your effectiveness and impact. Understanding the importance of influence in the workplace lays the foundation for success in achieving your objectives and advancing your career.

2. Types of Influence in Professional Settings

Influence manifests in various forms in professional settings, each with its dynamics and implications. From formal authority to informal persuasion, understanding the different types of influence empowers individuals to leverage their strengths and navigate power dynamics effectively. Exploring these types of influence provides valuable insights into how to exert influence strategically and ethically in professional contexts.

3. Strategies for Building Influence

Building influence in the workplace requires a combination of strategic thinking, interpersonal skills, and credibility. By adopting proven strategies for building influence, individuals can enhance their ability to sway opinions, shape decisions, and drive change. These strategies encompass cultivating relationships, demonstrating expertise, fostering trust, and leading by example to establish a strong foundation of influence in professional settings.

4. Overcoming Challenges to Influence

Influence is not without its challenges, as individuals may encounter resistance, skepticism, or competing interests in their efforts to exert influence. Overcoming these challenges requires resilience, adaptability, and effective communication. By understanding common obstacles to influence and developing strategies to address them, individuals can navigate setbacks and maintain momentum in achieving their goals.

5. Ethical Considerations in Influence

Ethical considerations are paramount in the exercise of influence, ensuring that individuals wield their power responsibly and ethically. Upholding ethical standards promotes trust, credibility, and integrity in professional interactions, fostering positive relationships and long-term success. Exploring ethical considerations in influence helps individuals navigate moral dilemmas and uphold their principles while pursuing their objectives.

6. Case Studies: Successful Influence in Action

Examining real-world case studies of successful influence in professional settings provides valuable insights into effective strategies and tactics. By analyzing examples of influential leaders, negotiators, and change agents, individuals can glean lessons and best practices for exerting influence in their careers. Case studies illuminate the dynamics of influence and offer practical guidance for achieving desired outcomes in diverse professional contexts.

Influence is a potent force in professional settings, shaping interactions, decisions, and outcomes in the workplace. By understanding its importance, mastering different types of influence, deploying effective strategies, overcoming challenges, and upholding ethical standards, individuals can harness the power of influence to achieve their goals and drive success in their careers. With careful consideration and strategic action, influence becomes a valuable tool for navigating the complexities of the modern workplace and making a meaningful impact in professional settings.

6.1 Influencing Colleagues and Superiors

Influencing colleagues and superiors is a key aspect of success in the workplace, enabling individuals to collaborate effectively, gain support for their ideas, and advance their careers. Understanding how to navigate relationships and exert influence in professional settings is essential for achieving goals and driving organizational success.

Understanding Colleagues and Superiors

To influence colleagues and superiors effectively, it's crucial to understand their perspectives, priorities, and communication styles. Take the time to build relationships and foster open communication channels, allowing you to gain insights into their motivations, concerns, and decision-making processes.

Building Trust and Credibility

Building trust and credibility is foundational to influencing colleagues and superiors. Demonstrate reliability, integrity, and competence in your work, consistently delivering high-quality results and fulfilling your commitments. Be transparent and honest in your interactions, fostering trust and confidence in your abilities.

Communicating Persuasively

Effective communication is essential for persuading colleagues and superiors to support your ideas and initiatives. Tailor your messages to resonate with their interests and priorities, highlighting the benefits and value of your proposals. Use persuasive techniques such as storytelling, data-driven arguments, and compelling visuals to make your case effectively.

Collaborating and Building Coalitions

Collaboration and coalition-building are powerful strategies for influencing colleagues and superiors. Identify common goals and areas of mutual interest, and work collaboratively to achieve shared objectives. Build alliances and networks within the organization, leveraging the support and influence of key stakeholders to advance your agenda.

Leveraging Influence Tactics

Deploying influence tactics can help sway opinions and gain buy-in from colleagues and superiors. Use strategies such as social proof, reciprocity, and scarcity to influence decision-making and encourage action. Adapt your approach based on the preferences and personalities of individuals, employing tactics that resonate with their motivations and concerns.

Managing Resistance and Conflict

Addressing resistance and conflict is an inevitable part of influencing colleagues and superiors. Approach disagreements with professionalism and respect, seeking to understand opposing viewpoints and find common ground. Use active listening and empathy to defuse tensions and foster constructive dialogue, ultimately finding win-win solutions that benefit all parties involved.

Seeking Feedback and Continuous Improvement

Seeking feedback and continuous improvement is essential for refining your approach to influencing colleagues and superiors. Solicit input from others on your communication style, strategies, and effectiveness in influencing outcomes. Be open to constructive criticism and use it as an opportunity for growth and development in your influence skills.

Influencing colleagues and superiors is a dynamic and nuanced process that requires empathy, communication skills, and strategic thinking. By understanding their perspectives, building trust and credibility, communicating persuasively, collaborating effectively, leveraging influence tactics, managing resistance and conflict, and seeking feedback for continuous improvement, individuals can exert positive influence in the workplace and achieve their professional objectives. With practice and perseverance, mastering the art of influencing colleagues and superiors becomes a valuable asset for success in any organizational setting.

6.2 Navigating Office Politics

Office politics are an inevitable aspect of workplace dynamics, involving the informal power struggles, alliances, and rivalries that influence decision-making and relationships within an organization. Navigating office politics effectively requires a combination of emotional intelligence, strategic thinking, and interpersonal skills to maintain professionalism and achieve objectives amidst complex social dynamics.

Understanding Office Politics

To navigate office politics successfully, it's essential to understand the underlying dynamics at play within the organization. Recognize the key players, power structures, and informal networks that shape decision-making and influence outcomes. Be mindful of office gossip, rumors, and hidden agendas, and seek to maintain a balanced perspective on interpersonal relationships and organizational dynamics.

Building Relationships Wisely

Building positive relationships with colleagues and stakeholders is crucial for navigating office politics. Cultivate genuine connections based on mutual respect, trust, and collaboration, rather than solely focusing on advancing your agenda. Invest time in networking and relationship-building activities, seeking opportunities to connect with individuals across different departments and levels of the organization.

Avoiding Gossip and Drama

Avoiding gossip and drama is essential for maintaining professionalism and credibility in the workplace. Refrain from participating in negative conversations or spreading rumors about colleagues, as this can damage relationships and undermine trust. Focus on constructive communication and positive interactions, steering clear of office politics that detract from your professional reputation.

Staying Neutral and Diplomatic

Staying neutral and diplomatic in office interactions is key to navigating complex social dynamics effectively. Refrain from taking sides in conflicts or power struggles, and avoid aligning yourself too closely with any particular individual or faction. Maintain a balanced perspective and approach interpersonal relationships with empathy, professionalism, and discretion.

Managing Conflicts and Disagreements

Managing conflicts and disagreements with colleagues requires tact, empathy, and assertiveness. Approach conflicts constructively, seeking to understand the underlying issues and perspectives of all parties involved. Use active listening and communication skills to facilitate dialogue and find mutually beneficial solutions that address the root causes of conflict.

Upholding Professionalism and Integrity

Upholding professionalism and integrity is paramount in navigating office politics with grace and integrity. Maintain high ethical standards in your conduct, adhering to company policies and values even in challenging situations. Demonstrate honesty, transparency, and fairness in your interactions, earning the trust and respect of your colleagues and superiors.

Focusing on Goals and Results

Focusing on goals and results helps to navigate office politics by keeping the focus on shared objectives and organizational success. Stay focused on your professional responsibilities and priorities, striving to deliver high-quality work and achieve measurable results. By demonstrating competence and commitment to excellence, you can earn recognition and credibility in the workplace, regardless of political dynamics.

Seeking Guidance and Support

Seeking guidance and support from mentors, trusted colleagues, or HR professionals can provide valuable insights and advice for navigating office politics. Reach out to experienced individuals who can offer perspective and guidance on complex workplace situations, helping you navigate challenges and make informed decisions.

Navigating office politics requires a combination of emotional intelligence, strategic thinking, and interpersonal skills to navigate complex social dynamics effectively. By understanding office politics, building positive relationships, avoiding gossip and drama, staying neutral and diplomatic, managing conflicts and disagreements, upholding professionalism and integrity, focusing on goals and results, and seeking guidance and support when needed, individuals can navigate office politics with grace and integrity, maintaining professionalism and achieving success in their careers. With self-awareness and resilience, mastering the art of navigating office politics becomes a valuable skill for thriving in any organizational environment.

6.3 Negotiation Tactics for Success

Negotiation is a fundamental skill in professional settings, enabling individuals to reach mutually beneficial agreements, resolve conflicts, and achieve their objectives. Success in negotiation requires a combination of strategic planning, effective communication, and interpersonal skills. In this section, we will explore negotiation tactics that can lead to successful outcomes in various workplace scenarios.

Preparation and Planning

Effective negotiation begins with thorough preparation and planning. Take the time to clarify your objectives, priorities, and desired outcomes before entering into negotiations. Research the relevant facts, data, and information to support your position, and anticipate potential challenges or objections that may arise during the negotiation process.

Establishing Common Ground

Establishing common ground with the other party is essential for building rapport and fostering a collaborative negotiation environment. Find areas of agreement or shared interests that can serve as a foundation for productive dialogue. By demonstrating empathy and understanding, you can create a positive atmosphere that facilitates open communication and problem-solving.

Setting Clear Goals and Boundaries

Setting clear goals and boundaries helps to guide the negotiation process and prevent misunderstandings or misinterpretations. Communicate your objectives, expectations, and limits to the other party, and be firm in asserting your interests while remaining flexible and open to compromise. Establishing clear parameters ensures that both parties have a shared understanding of the negotiation objectives and constraints.

Active Listening and Empathetic Communication

Active listening and empathetic communication are essential skills for effective negotiation. Listen attentively to the other party's concerns, interests, and perspectives, and demonstrate empathy and understanding for their position. Use reflective listening techniques to acknowledge their points and validate their feelings, fostering trust and rapport in the negotiation process.

Assertiveness and Confidence

Assertiveness and confidence are crucial for advocating for your interests and asserting your position during negotiations. Clearly articulate your needs, preferences, and desired outcomes with conviction and confidence, while remaining respectful and professional in your communication. Projecting confidence instills trust and credibility in your negotiation stance, increasing the likelihood of achieving favorable outcomes.

Creative Problem-Solving

Creative problem-solving involves exploring innovative solutions and alternatives to address the interests and concerns of both parties in negotiations. Brainstorm creative ideas and options that maximize value and benefit for both sides and be open to unconventional approaches or compromises that may lead to mutually beneficial agreements. By thinking outside the box and embracing flexibility, you can overcome impasses and find win-win solutions in negotiations.

Managing Emotions and Stress

Managing emotions and stress is essential for maintaining composure and professionalism during negotiations. Stay calm, composed, and focused on the negotiation objectives, even in challenging or high-pressure situations. Practice relaxation techniques, such as deep breathing or mindfulness, to manage stress and maintain clarity of thought and decision-making.

Building Trust and Rapport

Building trust and rapport with the other party is critical for fostering a positive negotiation environment and achieving successful outcomes. Demonstrate integrity, honesty, and transparency in your interactions, and follow through on your commitments and promises. By building trust and rapport, you can create a foundation of mutual respect and collaboration that facilitates effective negotiation and conflict resolution.

Flexibility and Adaptability

Flexibility and adaptability are essential for responding to changing circumstances or unexpected developments during negotiations. Be prepared to adjust your approach, tactics, or priorities as needed to accommodate the evolving dynamics of the negotiation process. By remaining flexible and adaptable, you can navigate obstacles and challenges more effectively and achieve favorable outcomes in negotiations.

Negotiation is a dynamic and multifaceted process that requires careful planning, effective communication, and strategic thinking to achieve successful outcomes. By employing tactics such as preparation and planning, establishing common ground, setting clear goals and boundaries, active listening and empathetic communication, assertiveness, and confidence, creative problem-solving, managing emotions and stress, building trust and rapport, flexibility and adaptability, individuals can negotiate with confidence and achieve their objectives in various workplace scenarios. With practice and perseverance, mastering the art of negotiation becomes a valuable skill for advancing careers, resolving conflicts, and driving success in professional settings.

Chapter 7: Influence in Personal Relationships

Influence is not limited to professional settings; it also plays a significant role in personal relationships, shaping interactions, decisions, and dynamics between individuals. Understanding how to wield influence effectively in personal relationships can foster deeper connections, resolve conflicts, and nurture healthy and fulfilling bonds. In this chapter, we will explore the dynamics of influence in personal relationships and strategies for building strong and positive connections with others.

1. The Importance of Influence in Personal Relationships

Influence is essential for fostering meaningful connections and navigating the complexities of personal relationships. Whether with family members, friends, romantic partners, or peers, the ability to influence others can strengthen bonds, resolve conflicts, and build trust and understanding. Understanding the importance of influence in personal relationships empowers individuals to communicate effectively and nurture strong and lasting connections with others.

2. Types of Influence in Personal Relationships

Influence manifests in various forms in personal relationships, each with its dynamics and implications. From persuasion to negotiation, understanding the different types of influence enables individuals to navigate interpersonal dynamics and achieve desired outcomes in their relationships. Exploring these types of influence provides insights into how to foster positive interactions and communicate effectively with loved ones.

3. Strategies for Building Influence in Personal Relationships

Building influence in personal relationships requires empathy, communication skills, and emotional intelligence. By employing strategies such as active listening, empathy, vulnerability, and compromise, individuals can strengthen connections and foster trust and mutual respect with their loved ones. These strategies empower individuals to navigate conflicts, express their needs, and nurture healthy and fulfilling relationships.

4. Nurturing Trust and Connection

Trust and connection are foundational to healthy and fulfilling relationships. By nurturing trust and connection through open communication, honesty, and authenticity, individuals can deepen their bonds with loved ones and create a supportive and nurturing environment. Building trust and connection fosters intimacy, empathy, and understanding, strengthening the foundation of personal relationships.

5. Resolving Conflicts and Overcoming Challenges

Conflicts and challenges are inevitable in personal relationships, but they also present opportunities for growth and deeper connection. By employing conflict resolution skills, such as active listening, empathy, and compromise, individuals can navigate disagreements and conflicts constructively, strengthening their relationships in the process. Overcoming challenges together builds resilience and fosters a sense of unity and partnership in personal relationships.

6. Communicating Effectively and Empathetically

Effective communication is essential for building influence and fostering healthy relationships. By communicating openly, honestly, and empathetically, individuals can express their thoughts, feelings, and needs authentically, fostering understanding and connection with their loved ones. Effective communication strengthens bonds and builds trust, laying the groundwork for positive and fulfilling relationships.

7. Balancing Power Dynamics and Autonomy

Balancing power dynamics and autonomy is crucial for maintaining healthy and equitable relationships. By respecting each other's autonomy, boundaries, and individuality, individuals can create a sense of equality and mutual respect in their relationships. Avoiding control or manipulation and fostering independence and agency allows for greater harmony and balance in personal relationships.

8. Cultivating Empathy and Understanding

Cultivating empathy and understanding is essential for building strong and empathetic relationships. By putting oneself in the shoes of others, individuals can gain insight into their perspectives, feelings, and experiences, fostering empathy and compassion in their relationships. Cultivating empathy and understanding promotes mutual support, validation, and emotional connection, enriching personal relationships.

9. Fostering Growth and Development

Personal relationships provide opportunities for growth, learning, and self-discovery. By supporting each other's personal growth and development, individuals can cultivate a sense of partnership and collaboration in their relationships. Encouraging each other's aspirations, goals, and interests fosters a sense of mutual support and empowerment, strengthening the bond between loved ones.

Influence is a powerful force in personal relationships, shaping interactions, decisions, and dynamics between individuals. By understanding the importance of influence, employing strategies for building influence, nurturing trust and connection, resolving conflicts, communicating effectively and empathetically, balancing power dynamics and autonomy, cultivating empathy and understanding, and fostering growth and development, individuals can nurture strong and fulfilling relationships with their loved ones. With care, empathy, and communication, mastering the art of influence in personal relationships becomes a pathway to deeper connection, mutual support, and lasting happiness.

7.1 Building Strong Relationships through Influence

Building strong relationships through influence is essential for fostering deep connections, trust, and mutual understanding with loved ones.

Whether with family members, friends, or romantic partners, the ability to positively influence others can strengthen bonds and create a supportive and nurturing environment. In this section, we will explore strategies for building strong relationships through influence.

1. Establishing Trust and Rapport

Trust and rapport are the foundation of strong relationships. Building trust involves demonstrating reliability, honesty, and integrity in your interactions with others. By consistently following through on your commitments, being transparent about your intentions, and showing genuine care and concern for the well-being of others, you can establish trust and rapport that form the basis of strong and lasting relationships.

2. Communicating with Empathy and Understanding

Effective communication is essential for building strong relationships. Communicate with empathy and understanding, seeking to understand the perspectives, feelings, and needs of your loved ones. Practice active listening, validate their experiences, and express empathy and compassion in your responses. By communicating with empathy and understanding, you can foster deeper connections and strengthen the bond with your loved ones.

3. Expressing Appreciation and Gratitude

Expressing appreciation and gratitude is a powerful way to strengthen relationships and cultivate positive feelings between individuals. Take the time to acknowledge and celebrate the contributions, qualities, and efforts of your loved ones. Express gratitude for their presence in your life and how they enrich your experiences. By expressing appreciation and gratitude, you can reinforce the value of your relationships and foster a sense of mutual respect and admiration.

4. Being Supportive and Empowering

Supporting and empowering your loved ones is essential for building strong and resilient relationships. Offer your encouragement, assistance, and guidance when needed, and empower them to pursue their goals, dreams, and aspirations. Be a source of strength and encouragement during challenging times, and celebrate their successes and achievements. By being supportive and empowering, you can create a nurturing and empowering environment that strengthens the bond with your loved ones.

5. Resolving Conflicts Constructively

Conflicts are a natural part of any relationship, but how they are resolved can either strengthen or weaken the bond between individuals. Approach conflicts with an open mind and a willingness to find mutually beneficial solutions. Practice active listening, empathy, and compromise, and avoid blame or defensiveness. By resolving conflicts constructively, you can deepen understanding, foster forgiveness, and strengthen the resilience of your relationships.

6. Setting and Respecting Boundaries

Setting and respecting boundaries is essential for maintaining healthy and respectful relationships. Communicate your needs, preferences, and limits, and respect the boundaries of your loved ones in return. Create a safe and supportive environment where everyone feels heard, valued, and respected. By setting and respecting boundaries, you can build trust, promote autonomy, and strengthen the foundation of your relationships.

7. Sharing Quality Time and Experiences

Sharing quality time and experiences with your loved ones is vital for building strong and meaningful connections. Make an effort to spend quality time together, engaging in activities and conversations that foster connection and intimacy. Create shared memories and experiences that deepen your bond and strengthen your relationship over time. By prioritizing quality time together, you can nurture the connection and create a sense of belonging and togetherness.

Building strong relationships through influence requires intentionality, empathy, and effort. By establishing trust and rapport, communicating with empathy and understanding, expressing appreciation and gratitude, being supportive and empowering, resolving conflicts constructively, setting and respecting boundaries, and sharing quality time and experiences, you can cultivate deep and meaningful connections with your loved ones. With care and commitment, mastering the art of influence in personal relationships becomes a pathway to greater intimacy, trust, and happiness in your relationships.

7.2 Resolving Conflicts Peacefully

Conflict is a natural part of relationships, but how it is handled can either strengthen or weaken the bond between individuals. Resolving conflicts peacefully requires effective communication, empathy, and a willingness to find mutually beneficial solutions. In this section, we will explore strategies for resolving conflicts peacefully in personal relationships.

1. Approach with Calmness and Respect

When conflicts arise, approach the situation with calmness and respect. Avoid escalating tensions by reacting impulsively or defensively. Take a moment to compose yourself and approach the conversation with an open mind and a willingness to listen. Show respect for the other person's perspective, even if you disagree with it.

2. Practice Active Listening

Active listening is essential for understanding the underlying issues and emotions driving the conflict. Listen attentively to the other person's concerns, without interrupting or judging. Show empathy and validation by paraphrasing their words and reflecting their feelings to them. By demonstrating that you understand their perspective, you can build trust and rapport in the conversation.

3. Communicate Assertively and Clearly

Communicate your thoughts and feelings assertively and clearly, using "I" statements to express your perspective without blaming or accusing the other person. Be honest and direct about how the conflict has impacted you and what you need to resolve it. Avoid making assumptions or generalizations, and focus on specific behaviors or actions that are causing tension.

4. Seek Common Ground

Find areas of agreement or shared interests that can serve as a foundation for finding common ground. Look for solutions that prioritize the needs and interests of both parties, rather than focusing solely on winning or being right. Brainstorm creative ideas and compromises that address the underlying concerns of both parties and lead to a mutually beneficial resolution.

5. Focus on the Issue, Not the Person

Keep the focus of the conversation on the specific issue at hand, rather than attacking or criticizing the other person personally. Separate the behavior from the individual, and avoid making sweeping judgments or character assessments. By focusing on the issue, you can work together to find solutions without damaging the relationship.

6. Practice Forgiveness and Letting Go

Forgiveness is a powerful tool for resolving conflicts and moving forward in relationships. Let go of resentment, grudges, and past grievances, and focus on finding solutions that promote healing and reconciliation. Recognize that everyone makes mistakes and deserves a second chance, and be willing to forgive and move on from the conflict.

7. Collaborate on Solutions

Collaborate with the other person to brainstorm and evaluate potential solutions to the conflict. Explore different options and compromises that address the needs and concerns of both parties. Be willing to be flexible and open-minded in your approach, and focus on finding win-win solutions that benefit everyone involved.

8. Follow Through on Agreements

Once a resolution has been reached, follow through on any agreements or commitments made during the conflict resolution process. Hold yourself and the other person accountable for implementing the agreed-upon solutions and making positive changes moving forward. Regularly check in with each other to ensure that the conflict has been fully resolved and that both parties are satisfied with the outcome.

Resolving conflicts peacefully requires patience, empathy, and effective communication skills. By approaching conflicts with calmness and respect, practicing active listening, communicating assertively and, seeking common ground, focusing on the issue, not the person, practicing forgiveness and letting go, collaborating on solutions, and following through on agreements, individuals can navigate conflicts in personal relationships with grace and maturity. With a commitment to understanding and cooperation, conflicts can be opportunities for growth, understanding, and strengthening the bond between individuals.

7.3 Persuasive Techniques in Parenting and Family Dynamics

Persuasion plays a vital role in parenting and family dynamics, influencing children's behavior, fostering cooperation, and strengthening family bonds. Effective persuasion techniques can help parents communicate expectations, instill values, and resolve conflicts positively and constructively. In this section, we will explore persuasive techniques that parents can employ to promote harmony and mutual understanding in their families.

1. Positive Reinforcement

Positive reinforcement involves praising and rewarding desirable behavior, encouraging children to repeat it in the future. By highlighting and celebrating their achievements and efforts, parents can reinforce positive behaviors and values in their children. Positive reinforcement fosters a supportive and nurturing environment, where children feel valued and motivated to meet expectations.

2. Setting Clear Expectations

Setting clear expectations and boundaries provides children with structure and guidance, helping them understand what is expected of them. Communicate rules, responsibilities, and consequences calmly and consistently. By setting clear expectations, parents empower children to make informed choices and take responsibility for their actions.

3. Leading by Example

Leading by example is a powerful persuasive technique that parents can use to influence their children's behavior and attitudes. Model the values, behaviors, and habits that you want to instill in your children, such as kindness, honesty, and respect. Children learn by observing and imitating their parents, so strive to be a positive role model in all aspects of your life.

4. Active Listening

Active listening involves fully engaging with your children's thoughts, feelings, and concerns, demonstrating empathy and understanding. Listen attentively to their perspectives without judgment or interruption, and validate their feelings and experiences. By showing genuine interest and empathy, parents can build trust and rapport with their children, strengthening the parent-child bond.

5. Providing Logical Reasons

Providing logical reasons for rules and decisions helps children understand the rationale behind them, making them more likely to comply. Explain the reasons behind your expectations and decisions in a clear and age-appropriate manner, emphasizing the benefits and consequences involved. By involving children in the decision-making process and providing logical explanations, parents can promote understanding and cooperation.

6. Offering Choices

Offering choices empowers children to make decisions and take ownership of their actions, fostering independence and autonomy. Present options and alternatives whenever possible, allowing children to express their preferences and exercise control over their lives. By offering choices within reasonable limits, parents can promote self-confidence and decision-making skills in their children.

7. Using Positive Language

Using positive language when communicating with children helps maintain a supportive and encouraging atmosphere. Avoid negative or critical language, and instead focus on praising effort, highlighting strengths, and offering encouragement. Positive language fosters self-esteem and resilience in children, motivating them to strive for success and persevere through challenges.

8. Collaborative Problem-Solving

Collaborative problem-solving involves working together with children to find solutions to conflicts and challenges. Encourage open dialogue and brainstorming, allowing children to express their thoughts and feelings freely. By involving children in the problem-solving process and considering their perspectives, parents can promote critical thinking skills and conflict resolution abilities in their children.

Persuasive techniques play a crucial role in parenting and family dynamics, shaping children's behavior, attitudes, and values. By employing positive reinforcement, setting clear expectations, leading by example, practicing active listening, providing logical reasons, offering choices, using positive language, and promoting collaborative problem-solving, parents can effectively influence their children's behavior and foster harmonious and supportive family relationships. With patience, empathy, and consistency, parents can create a nurturing and empowering environment where children thrive and flourish.

Chapter 8: Ethical Considerations in Influence

Influence is a powerful tool that can be used to shape opinions, behaviors, and outcomes in various contexts. However, with this power comes the responsibility to wield it ethically and responsibly. In this chapter, we will explore the ethical considerations involved in influence and how individuals can ensure that their actions align with moral principles and values.

1. Understanding Ethical Influence

Ethical influence involves using persuasion, manipulation, or coercion in a manner that is morally upright and respectful of others' rights and autonomy. It requires individuals to consider the impact of their actions on others and to prioritize honesty, integrity, and fairness in their interactions. Understanding the principles of ethical influence lays the foundation for responsible and conscientious behavior.

2. Honesty and Transparency

Honesty and transparency are fundamental ethical principles that should guide all forms of influence. Individuals should be truthful and forthcoming in their communications, avoiding deception, exaggeration, or misrepresentation of facts. By being transparent about their intentions, motives, and interests, individuals can build trust and credibility with others, fostering genuine and authentic relationships.

3. Respecting Autonomy and Consent

Respecting autonomy and consent is essential in ethical influence, as it acknowledges individuals' right to make their own choices and decisions. Individuals should seek informed consent before attempting to influence others, ensuring that they understand the potential consequences of their actions and have the freedom to accept or reject them. Respecting autonomy promotes dignity, respect, and empowerment in interpersonal interactions.

4. Avoiding Manipulation and Coercion

Manipulation and coercion have no place in ethical influence, as they involve exploiting others' vulnerabilities or exerting undue pressure to achieve desired outcomes. Individuals should refrain from using manipulative tactics or coercive strategies to influence others, instead focusing on building consensus, fostering collaboration, and respecting others' boundaries. Avoiding manipulation and coercion upholds the principles of autonomy, dignity, and respect for others' rights.

5. Promoting Well-Being and Beneficence

Promoting well-being and beneficence is a key ethical consideration in influence, as it involves prioritizing the welfare and best interests of others. Individuals should strive to influence others in ways that promote positive outcomes, enhance their quality of life, and contribute to their flourishing. By considering the potential impact of their actions on others' well-being, individuals can ensure that their influence aligns with ethical principles of beneficence and compassion.

6. Upholding Integrity and Professionalism

Upholding integrity and professionalism is essential for maintaining ethical standards in influence. Individuals should adhere to ethical codes of conduct and professional standards in their interactions, avoiding conflicts of interest, unethical practices, or behaviors that undermine trust and credibility. By acting with integrity and professionalism, individuals can inspire confidence and respect in their influence efforts, fostering positive relationships and outcomes.

7. Balancing Persuasion and Respect

Balancing persuasion and respect is a delicate ethical consideration in influence, as it involves advocating for one's interests while respecting the autonomy and dignity of others. Individuals should strive to persuade others through reasoned arguments, evidence-based reasoning, and respectful dialogue, rather than resorting to manipulation or coercion. By finding a balance between persuasion and respect, individuals can influence others in ways that are both effective and ethical.

8. Reflecting on Consequences and Accountability

Reflecting on the consequences of one's influence actions and taking accountability for their impact is crucial in ethical decision-making.

Individuals should consider the potential ramifications of their influence efforts on others and society as a whole, weighing the benefits and risks of their actions. Taking responsibility for the outcomes of their influence can help individuals mitigate harm, rectify unintended consequences, and uphold ethical principles in their interactions.

Ethical considerations are paramount in influencing and guiding individuals to wield their power responsibly and respectfully. By prioritizing honesty and transparency, respecting autonomy and consent, avoiding manipulation and coercion, promoting well-being and beneficence, upholding integrity and professionalism, balancing persuasion and respect, and reflecting on consequences and accountability, individuals can ensure that their influence aligns with moral principles and values. With mindfulness, integrity, and empathy, ethical influence becomes a force for positive change and ethical leadership in interpersonal interactions and societal contexts.

8.1 Ethical Guidelines for Persuasion

When engaging in persuasion, it's crucial to adhere to ethical guidelines to ensure that your actions are respectful, honest, and responsible. Ethical persuasion involves influencing others in a manner that upholds their dignity, autonomy, and well-being. In this section, we will outline ethical guidelines to follow when persuading others:

1. Respect Autonomy and Consent

Respect the autonomy and freedom of choice of the individuals you seek to persuade. Obtain informed consent before attempting to influence them, ensuring that they understand the implications of their decisions and have the opportunity to accept or decline your proposal willingly.

2. Be Honest and Transparent

Maintain honesty and transparency in your communications and interactions. Present information accurately and truthfully, avoiding exaggeration, omission, or distortion of facts. Be upfront about your intentions, motives, and interests, fostering trust and credibility in your persuasive efforts.

3. Avoid Manipulation and Coercion

Refrain from using manipulative tactics or coercion to persuade others. Respect their autonomy and right to make their own decisions, without exerting undue pressure or exploiting their vulnerabilities. Focus on presenting reasoned arguments and providing relevant information, rather than resorting to deceptive or unethical tactics.

4. Prioritize Well-Being and Beneficence

Prioritize the well-being and best interests of the individuals you seek to persuade. Ensure that your persuasive efforts contribute to their welfare, enhance their quality of life, and promote positive outcomes. Consider the potential impact of your actions on their emotional, psychological, and physical well-being.

5. Uphold Integrity and Professionalism

Maintain integrity and professionalism in your persuasive endeavors. Adhere to ethical codes of conduct and professional standards, avoiding conflicts of interest, dishonesty, or unethical behavior. Act with honesty, integrity, and respect for others' rights and dignity at all times.

6. Foster Open Dialogue and Collaboration

Foster open dialogue and collaboration in your persuasive interactions. Encourage individuals to express their thoughts, concerns, and preferences openly, and listen attentively to their perspectives. Engage in respectful and constructive dialogue, seeking to understand their viewpoints and find common ground.

7. Respect Cultural and Individual Differences

Respect cultural diversity and individual differences in your persuasive efforts. Recognize that individuals may have unique values, beliefs, and preferences shaped by their cultural background, upbringing, and experiences. Tailor your persuasive approach to accommodate their cultural norms and individual preferences, fostering mutual respect and understanding.

8. Reflect on Consequences and Accountability

Reflect on the potential consequences of your persuasive actions and take accountability for their impact. Consider the short-term and long-term implications of your influence efforts on individuals, relationships, and society as a whole. Take responsibility for any unintended consequences and strive to rectify harm or mitigate negative outcomes.

Ethical persuasion requires a commitment to respecting autonomy, honesty, integrity, and well-being in all persuasive interactions. By following these ethical guidelines, individuals can ensure that their persuasive efforts are conducted responsibly, respectfully, and ethically. With mindfulness and integrity, ethical persuasion becomes a force for positive change and constructive communication in personal and professional relationships.

8.2 Recognizing and Avoiding Manipulation

Manipulation is a deceptive and unethical tactic used to influence others without their informed consent or in a way that undermines their autonomy and well-being. It can take various forms, such as emotional manipulation, gaslighting, guilt-tripping, or exploitation of vulnerabilities. Recognizing and avoiding manipulation is essential for maintaining healthy relationships and upholding ethical standards. In this section, we will discuss strategies for identifying and steering clear of manipulation:

1. Trust Your Instincts

Trust your instincts and intuition when interacting with others. If something feels off or manipulative, take a step back and reassess the situation. Pay attention to any feelings of discomfort, unease, or suspicion, as they may be warning signs of manipulation.

2. Question Motives and Intentions

Question the motives and intentions behind others' actions and requests. Consider whether their behavior aligns with your best interests or if they have ulterior motives. Be wary of individuals who seem overly controlling, manipulative, or insincere in their interactions.

3. Watch for Red Flags

Be vigilant for red flags that indicate manipulation, such as:

- Excessive flattery or praise followed by requests for favors.
- Persistent pressure or coercion to comply with demands.
- Guilt-tripping or emotional manipulation to evoke sympathy or compliance.
- Gaslighting tactics to distort reality or undermine your perception of events.
- Withholding information or providing misleading or incomplete details to manipulate your decisions.

4. Set Boundaries and Assert Yourself

Set clear boundaries and assert yourself when faced with manipulation. Communicate your limits and expectations firmly and assertively, refusing to be swayed or coerced into actions that compromise your values or well-being. Stand firm in defending your autonomy and rights.

5. Seek Feedback from Trusted Sources

Seek feedback from trusted friends, family members, or mentors if you're unsure whether you're being manipulated. Share your concerns and observations with them and ask for their perspective and advice. An outside perspective can provide valuable insights and help you see the situation more clearly.

6. Educate Yourself on Manipulative Tactics

Educate yourself on common manipulative tactics and techniques used by manipulators. By understanding how manipulation operates and recognizing its signs, you can better protect yourself from falling victim to manipulative behavior. Resources such as books, articles, or workshops on assertiveness and communication skills can be helpful in this regard.

7. Practice Self-Care and Self-Reflection

Practice self-care and self-reflection to maintain emotional resilience and self-awareness. Take time to check in with yourself regularly, identify any feelings of manipulation or coercion, and address them proactively. Engage in activities that promote self-esteem, confidence, and well-being.

8. Seek Support if Necessary

Seek support from a therapist, counselor, or support group if you've experienced manipulation or struggle to recognize and avoid manipulative behavior. Professional guidance can help you develop healthy coping strategies, assertiveness skills, and boundary-setting techniques to protect yourself from manipulation and maintain healthy relationships.

Recognizing and avoiding manipulation is essential for preserving autonomy, integrity, and well-being in relationships. By trusting your instincts, questioning motives, watching for red flags, setting boundaries, seeking feedback, educating yourself, practicing self-care, and seeking support when needed, you can protect yourself from manipulation and maintain healthy and respectful interactions with others. With mindfulness and assertiveness, you can navigate relationships with confidence and integrity, free from the influence of manipulative tactics.

8.3 Using Influence Responsibly

Influence is a powerful tool that can shape opinions, behaviors, and outcomes in various contexts. However, with this power comes the responsibility to wield it ethically, responsibly, and with consideration for others' well-being and autonomy. Using influence responsibly involves employing persuasion techniques in a manner that upholds moral principles, respects individuals' rights, and promotes positive outcomes. In this section, we will discuss strategies for using influence responsibly:

1. Prioritize Ethical Considerations

Prioritize ethical considerations in your use of influence, ensuring that your actions align with moral principles and values. Consider the potential impact of your influence efforts on others' well-being, autonomy, and rights. Uphold honesty, integrity, transparency, and respect for others in all your interactions and communications.

2. Respect Autonomy and Consent

Respect individuals' autonomy and right to make their own decisions. Obtain informed consent before attempting to influence them, ensuring that they understand the implications of their choices and have the freedom to accept or decline your proposal willingly. Avoid using manipulative tactics or coercion to sway their decisions.

3. Foster Collaboration and Dialogue

Foster collaboration and dialogue in your influence efforts, engaging others in respectful and constructive discussions. Listen attentively to their perspectives, concerns, and preferences, and seek common ground and mutually beneficial solutions. Encourage open communication, feedback, and participation to promote inclusivity and empowerment.

4. Promote Well-Being and Empowerment

Promote the well-being and empowerment of those you seek to influence. Ensure that your influence efforts contribute to their welfare, growth, and self-determination. Offer support, encouragement, and resources that enable them to make informed choices, achieve their goals, and fulfill their potential.

5. Lead by Example

Lead by example in your use of influence, demonstrating integrity, authenticity, and ethical behavior in all your actions and interactions. Be a positive role model for others to emulate, embodying the values and principles you wish to promote. Inspire trust, respect, and credibility through your consistent words and deeds.

6. Consider Long-Term Consequences

Consider the long-term consequences of your influence efforts on individuals, relationships, and society as a whole. Strive to achieve sustainable and positive outcomes that benefit not only the immediate stakeholders but also future generations. Take responsibility for any unintended consequences and work to mitigate harm or rectify negative impacts.

7. Continuously Evaluate and Reflect

Continuously evaluate and reflect on your use of influence, seeking feedback and self-assessment to improve your effectiveness and ethical conduct. Consider the feedback and perspectives of others, and be open to learning and growth. Regularly reassess your motives, methods, and outcomes to ensure that they align with your values and goals.

8. Act with Compassion and Empathy

Act with compassion and empathy in your influence efforts, recognizing the inherent worth and dignity of every individual. Consider their perspectives, feelings, and experiences with empathy and sensitivity, and strive to promote understanding, connection, and mutual respect. Treat others with kindness, fairness, and empathy, fostering a culture of trust and cooperation.

Using influence responsibly requires a commitment to ethical conduct, respect for autonomy, and consideration for others' well-being and rights. By prioritizing ethical considerations, respecting autonomy and consent, fostering collaboration and dialogue, promoting well-being and empowerment, leading by example, considering long-term consequences, continuously evaluating and reflecting, and acting with compassion and empathy, individuals can use their influence to effect positive change and create a more just, equitable, and compassionate world. With mindfulness, integrity, and compassion, responsible influence becomes a force for meaningful and sustainable impact in personal, professional, and societal contexts.

Chapter 9: Overcoming Resistance and Objections

Influence often encounters resistance and objections, presenting challenges that require skillful navigation to achieve desired outcomes. Overcoming resistance and objections involves understanding the underlying concerns, addressing them effectively, and fostering cooperation and agreement. In this chapter, we will explore strategies for overcoming resistance and objections in various contexts:

1. Understanding Resistance and Objections

Resistance and objections arise when individuals are reluctant to accept a proposed idea, change, or course of action. They may stem from concerns about the potential risks, consequences, or implications of the proposal, as well as personal biases, fears, or preferences. Understanding the root causes of resistance and objections is essential for devising effective strategies to address them.

2. Strategies for Overcoming Resistance and Objections

1. Active Listening

Practice active listening to understand the concerns and objections raised by others fully. Listen attentively to their perspectives, validate their feelings, and demonstrate empathy and understanding. By acknowledging their concerns and showing genuine interest in their viewpoints, you can build rapport and trust, paving the way for constructive dialogue and collaboration.

2. Addressing Concerns

Address the concerns and objections raised by others directly and transparently. Provide reassurance, clarification, or additional information to alleviate their worries and uncertainties. Be honest and forthcoming about any potential risks or drawbacks, and offer viable solutions or alternatives to mitigate them. By addressing concerns proactively, you can instill confidence and trust in your proposal.

3. Building Rapport and Trust

Build rapport and trust with the individuals you seek to influence, establishing a positive and supportive relationship. Invest time and effort in cultivating mutual respect, understanding, and cooperation. Show genuine interest in their well-being and success, and demonstrate reliability, integrity, and consistency in your actions. A strong foundation of trust and rapport can help overcome resistance and objections more effectively.

4. Framing the Message

Frame your message in a way that resonates with the concerns, values, and priorities of the individuals you are trying to influence. Tailor your communication to address their specific needs, preferences, and interests, highlighting the benefits and advantages of your proposal. Use persuasive language, compelling narratives, and concrete examples to illustrate the positive outcomes and opportunities associated with your ideas.

5. Anticipating and Preempting Objections

Anticipate potential objections and concerns before they arise, and preemptively address them in your communication. Anticipating objections demonstrates foresight and preparedness, and signals to others that you have considered their perspectives and are proactive in addressing their concerns. By addressing objections proactively, you can preemptively disarm skepticism and resistance.

6. Seeking Collaboration and Input

Seek collaboration and input from others in the decision-making process, inviting their participation and contributions. Encourage brainstorming, idea-sharing, and collaboration to generate creative solutions and alternatives. By involving others in the process, you demonstrate respect for their expertise and insights and foster a sense of ownership and investment in the outcome.

7. Patience and Persistence

Practice patience and persistence when faced with resistance and objections, recognizing that change and persuasion take time. Avoid becoming discouraged or disheartened by initial setbacks or pushback. Instead, remain resilient and committed to your goals, and continue to engage in constructive dialogue and problem-solving. With patience and persistence, you can gradually overcome resistance and objections and achieve meaningful progress.

Overcoming resistance and objections is a critical aspect of effective influence, requiring empathy, understanding, and strategic communication. By practicing active listening, addressing concerns, building rapport and trust, framing the message, anticipating objections, seeking collaboration and input, and demonstrating patience and persistence, individuals can navigate resistance and objections with skill and confidence. With a proactive and empathetic approach, resistance can be transformed into cooperation, and objections can become opportunities for dialogue and growth.

9.1 Strategies for Handling Resistance

Resistance is a natural response to change, new ideas, or proposals that challenge the status quo. Effectively handling resistance requires empathy, communication skills, and strategic approaches to address concerns and foster acceptance. In this section, we will explore strategies for handling resistance:

1. Acknowledge and Validate Concerns

Acknowledge and validate the concerns and feelings of those expressing resistance. Show empathy and understanding for their perspectives, demonstrating that you value their input and opinions. By acknowledging their concerns, you create a sense of psychological safety and open the door for constructive dialogue.

2. Communicate Openly and Transparently

Communicate openly and transparently about the reasons behind the proposed change or idea. Provide clear and honest explanations of the rationale, objectives, and expected benefits. Address any misconceptions or misunderstandings that may contribute to resistance, and ensure that individuals have access to accurate information.

3. Listen Actively and Empathetically

Listen actively and empathetically to the concerns and objections raised by individuals resisting change. Pay close attention to their perspectives, feelings, and underlying motivations. Validate their experiences and emotions, and demonstrate empathy by acknowledging their perspective without judgment.

4. Provide Opportunities for Input and Participation

Provide opportunities for individuals to contribute their ideas, feedback, and suggestions regarding the proposed change. Involve them in the decision-making process and seek their input on how the change can be implemented effectively. By empowering individuals to participate in the change process, you foster a sense of ownership and investment in the outcome.

5. Address Concerns Proactively

Address concerns and objections proactively by providing reassurance, clarification, or additional information as needed. Anticipate potential obstacles or challenges that may arise during the change process, and develop strategies to mitigate them in advance. By addressing concerns proactively, you demonstrate responsiveness and a commitment to addressing individuals' needs.

6. Highlight the Benefits and Opportunities

Highlight the benefits and opportunities associated with the proposed change or idea. Emphasize how it aligns with organizational goals, values, and priorities, and how it can contribute to individual and collective success. Provide concrete examples and success stories to illustrate the positive outcomes and opportunities that the change can bring.

7. Foster Collaboration and Support

Foster collaboration and support among individuals affected by the proposed change. Encourage teamwork, mutual support, and solidarity to navigate challenges and obstacles together. Create opportunities for individuals to share resources, expertise, and best practices to facilitate a smooth transition.

8. Be Patient and Persistent

Be patient and persistent in addressing resistance, recognizing that change takes time and effort. Avoid becoming discouraged by initial setbacks or resistance, and remain committed to engaging in ongoing dialogue and problem-solving. Demonstrate resilience and perseverance in pursuing the desired change outcomes.

Handling resistance requires empathy, communication skills, and strategic approaches to address concerns and foster acceptance. By acknowledging and validating concerns, communicating openly and transparently, listening actively and empathetically, providing opportunities for input and participation, addressing concerns proactively, highlighting benefits and opportunities, fostering collaboration and support, and being patient and persistent, individuals can navigate resistance effectively and achieve successful change outcomes. With empathy, patience, and strategic communication, resistance can be transformed into cooperation and acceptance, paving the way for positive organizational and personal growth.

9.2 Turning Objections into Opportunities

Objections are natural responses to new ideas, proposals, or changes, reflecting concerns, doubts, or uncertainties. Rather than viewing objections as barriers to progress, they can be seen as opportunities for dialogue, learning, and improvement. Turning objections into opportunities involves listening actively, addressing concerns effectively, and fostering collaboration to find mutually beneficial solutions. In this section, we will explore strategies for turning objections into opportunities:

1. Listen Actively and Empathetically

Listen actively and empathetically to the objections raised by individuals. Pay close attention to their concerns, perspectives, and underlying motivations. Demonstrate empathy and understanding by acknowledging their feelings and experiences without judgment. By listening attentively, you create a supportive environment for open dialogue and problem-solving.

2. Seek to Understand Root Causes

Seek to understand the root causes of objections by asking clarifying questions and engaging in reflective dialogue. Explore the reasons behind individuals' concerns, fears, or uncertainties, and uncover any underlying assumptions or beliefs that may influence their objections. By understanding the root causes, you can address objections more effectively and find common ground.

3. Address Concerns Effectively

Address objections effectively by providing reassurance, clarification, or additional information as needed. Offer evidence, data, or examples to support your arguments and alleviate doubts or misconceptions. Be transparent about any potential risks or drawbacks associated with the proposed idea or change, and discuss strategies to mitigate them. By addressing concerns proactively, you build trust and credibility with individuals.

4. Reframe Objections as Opportunities

Reframe objections as opportunities for dialogue, learning, and improvement. Encourage individuals to voice their objections openly and constructively, viewing them as valuable input for refining ideas and solutions. Shift the focus from resistance to collaboration, inviting individuals to contribute their perspectives and expertise to the discussion. By reframing objections as opportunities, you foster a culture of innovation and continuous improvement.

5. Explore Alternative Perspectives

Explore alternative perspectives and solutions to address objections creatively. Encourage brainstorming and idea-sharing to generate innovative approaches that accommodate diverse viewpoints and preferences. Collaborate with individuals to co-create solutions that meet their needs while aligning with organizational goals and objectives. By exploring alternative perspectives, you expand the range of possibilities and identify novel solutions to challenges.

6. Collaborate to Find Mutual Solutions

Collaborate with individuals to find mutually beneficial solutions that address their objections while advancing shared goals and interests. Foster teamwork, communication, and trust to facilitate collaborative problem-solving and decision-making. Encourage compromise and flexibility to accommodate differing priorities and preferences. By collaborating effectively, you create win-win outcomes that satisfy everyone involved.

7. Follow Up and Follow Through

Follow up and follow through on commitments made during the objection-handling process. Keep individuals informed of progress, updates, and next steps, and solicit feedback on the implementation of agreed-upon solutions. Demonstrate accountability and transparency in your actions, and address any outstanding concerns or issues promptly. By following up and following through, you reinforce trust and confidence in the decision-making process.

Turning objections into opportunities requires empathy, open-mindedness, and collaboration to address concerns constructively and find mutually beneficial solutions. By listening actively, understanding root causes, addressing concerns effectively, reframing objections as opportunities, exploring alternative perspectives, collaborating to find mutual solutions, and following up and following through, individuals can transform objections into catalysts for positive change and innovation. With a proactive and collaborative approach, objections become opportunities for growth, learning, and improvement, driving progress and success in personal and organizational endeavors.

9.3 Dealing with Skepticism and Doubt

Skepticism and doubt are natural responses to new ideas, proposals, or changes, reflecting individuals' cautiousness and critical thinking. Effectively dealing with skepticism and doubt requires patience, empathy, and persuasive communication to address concerns and build confidence in the proposed initiatives. In this section, we will explore strategies for dealing with skepticism and doubt:

1. Acknowledge and Validate Concerns

Acknowledge and validate the skepticism and doubts expressed by individuals. Show empathy and understanding for their perspectives, acknowledging that their cautiousness is a valid response to unfamiliar or uncertain situations. By validating their concerns, you create a supportive environment for open dialogue and collaboration.

2. Provide Clear and Transparent Communication

Provide clear and transparent communication about the rationale, objectives, and expected benefits of the proposed initiatives. Address any misconceptions or misunderstandings that may contribute to skepticism or doubt, and offer evidence, data, or examples to support your arguments. Be honest and upfront about any potential risks or challenges, and discuss strategies to mitigate them effectively.

3. Build Credibility and Trust

Build credibility and trust with individuals by demonstrating competence, reliability, and integrity in your actions and communications. Provide evidence of past successes or achievements that showcase your ability to deliver on promises and overcome challenges. Foster open and honest communication, and be responsive to individuals' concerns and feedback.

4. Engage in Active Listening

Engage in active listening to understand the underlying reasons for skepticism and doubt. Pay attention to individuals' concerns, perspectives, and motivations, and seek to uncover any underlying assumptions or beliefs that may influence their skepticism. By listening attentively, you demonstrate respect for their viewpoints and create opportunities for constructive dialogue.

5. Address Concerns Proactively

Address concerns proactively by providing reassurance, clarification, or additional information as needed. Anticipate potential objections or questions that may arise and prepare thoughtful responses in advance. Be transparent about the potential benefits and drawbacks of the proposed initiatives, and discuss strategies to maximize benefits and mitigate risks effectively.

6. Foster Collaboration and Participation

Foster collaboration and participation among individuals by involving them in the decision-making process and seeking their input on key issues. Encourage brainstorming, idea-sharing, and problem-solving to generate innovative solutions and approaches. By involving individuals in the process, you empower them to contribute their expertise and insights, fostering ownership and investment in the proposed initiatives.

7. Demonstrate Results and Progress

Demonstrate tangible results and progress to build confidence and credibility in the proposed initiatives. Provide regular updates and reports on the implementation of the initiatives, highlighting achievements, milestones, and successes. Celebrate successes and recognize individuals' contributions to reinforce their commitment and engagement.

8. Be Patient and Persistent

Be patient and persistent in addressing skepticism and doubt, recognizing that change takes time and effort. Avoid becoming discouraged by initial resistance or skepticism, and remain committed to engaging in ongoing dialogue and problem-solving. Demonstrate resilience and perseverance in pursuing the desired outcomes, and celebrate incremental progress along the way.

Dealing with skepticism and doubt requires empathy, communication skills, and strategic approaches to address concerns and build confidence in proposed initiatives. By acknowledging and validating concerns, providing clear and transparent communication, building credibility and trust, engaging in active listening, addressing concerns proactively, fostering collaboration and participation, demonstrating results and progress, and being patient and persistent, individuals can effectively navigate skepticism and doubt and achieve successful outcomes. With patience, empathy, and persuasive communication, skepticism can be transformed into confidence, paving the way for positive change and innovation in personal and organizational endeavors.

Chapter 10: Leveraging Social Influence

Social influence plays a pivotal role in shaping our thoughts, behaviors, and decisions in various aspects of life. Understanding how social influence operates and leveraging it effectively can empower individuals to achieve their goals, influence others positively, and foster meaningful connections. In this chapter, we will explore the dynamics of social influence and strategies for leveraging it to our advantage:

Understanding the Power of Social Influence

1. Social Norms and Conformity

Explore how social norms and the desire for conformity influence our behavior and decision-making. Discuss the factors that contribute to conformity, such as group pressure, social approval, and fear of rejection. Highlight the impact of social norms on shaping attitudes, beliefs, and actions within social groups.

2. Social Proof and Persuasion

Examine the concept of social proof and its role in persuasion and influence. Discuss how individuals look to others for cues on how to behave or what choices to make, particularly in ambiguous or uncertain situations. Explore strategies for leveraging social proof to influence behavior and foster acceptance of ideas or initiatives.

Harnessing Social Influence in Practice

1. Building Social Capital

Discuss the importance of building social capital – the network of relationships and connections that facilitate cooperation and collaboration. Explore strategies for expanding one's social network, cultivating meaningful relationships, and nurturing trust and reciprocity with others. Highlight the benefits of social capital in achieving personal and professional goals.

2. Influencing Through Social Networks

Explore how social networks can be leveraged to amplify influence and spread ideas or messages. Discuss the principles of network theory and how information or behaviors can spread through social ties. Highlight strategies for identifying key influencers within networks and engaging them to promote desired outcomes.

Ethical Considerations in Social Influence

1. Maintaining Integrity and Authenticity

Emphasize the importance of maintaining integrity and authenticity when leveraging social influence. Discuss the ethical implications of manipulating or exploiting social dynamics for personal gain. Encourage individuals to uphold honesty, transparency, and respect for others' autonomy and well-being in their influence efforts.

2. Respecting Diversity and Inclusion

Highlight the significance of respecting diversity and inclusion in social influence endeavors. Discuss how cultural differences, social identities, and perspectives shape individuals' responses to influence attempts. Encourage sensitivity to cultural norms, values, and preferences, and advocate for inclusive practices that honor and celebrate diversity.

Leveraging social influence effectively requires a nuanced understanding of social dynamics, ethical considerations, and strategic communication skills. By understanding the power of social norms and conformity, harnessing social influence in practice, and upholding ethical principles and values, individuals can leverage social influence to achieve their goals, foster positive change, and build meaningful connections in personal and professional spheres. With mindfulness, integrity, and empathy, social influence becomes a powerful force for building trust, driving collective action, and shaping a better future for individuals and communities alike.

10.1 Harnessing the Power of Social Proof

Social proof is a psychological phenomenon where people look to others to determine the correct behavior or decision in a given situation. It's a powerful tool for influencing behavior and shaping perceptions. Harnessing the power of social proof involves understanding how it works and strategically leveraging it to achieve desired outcomes. In this section, we will explore strategies for harnessing the power of social proof:

1. Cultivate Positive Social Proof

Strive to cultivate positive social proof by showcasing testimonials, reviews, or endorsements from satisfied customers, clients, or peers. Highlight success stories, testimonials, or case studies that demonstrate the benefits or effectiveness of your products, services, or ideas. By providing evidence of social approval and validation, you can bolster credibility and trustworthiness.

2. Showcase Social Influence

Showcase social influence by highlighting the popularity or acceptance of your offerings within relevant social groups or communities. Display social media metrics, such as likes, shares, or followers, to demonstrate social validation and endorsement. Leverage influencers or thought leaders within your industry or niche to endorse your brand or message, amplifying your reach and credibility.

3. Encourage User-generated Content

Encourage user-generated content by inviting customers or followers to share their experiences, testimonials, or reviews on social media platforms or review sites. Create opportunities for user engagement and participation, such as contests, challenges, or interactive campaigns that encourage sharing and social validation. By empowering users to become advocates for your brand or message, you can harness the power of peer influence.

4. Leverage Social Proof Tools

Utilize social proof tools and tactics, such as social proof notifications, testimonials widgets, or real-time activity feeds, to create a sense of urgency and social validation. Showcase recent purchases, sign-ups, or interactions to convey popularity and demand. Implement social proof strategies, such as scarcity or urgency messaging, to prompt action and increase conversions.

5. Align with Social Norms

Align your messaging and offerings with prevailing social norms and behaviors to enhance their appeal and acceptance. Highlight how your products, services, or ideas align with commonly held values, beliefs, or aspirations within your target audience. Frame your messaging in a way that emphasizes social acceptance or conformity, tapping into the desire to fit in or belong.

6. Foster Social Communities

Foster social communities or tribes around your brand, message, or cause to create a sense of belonging and camaraderie among followers. Encourage interaction, collaboration, and support within the community, facilitating peer-to-peer engagement and validation. By nurturing a sense of community ownership and identity, you can amplify social proof and influence within your network.

7. Monitor and Adapt

Monitor social proof indicators, such as engagement metrics, customer feedback, or market trends, to assess the effectiveness of your strategies and make adjustments as needed. Continuously evaluate the impact of social proof tactics on audience perception, behavior, and outcomes, and refine your approach based on feedback and insights. Stay agile and adaptable in responding to changes in social dynamics and audience preferences.

Harnessing the power of social proof requires strategic planning, creativity, and responsiveness to social dynamics. By cultivating positive social proof, showcasing social influence, encouraging user-generated content, leveraging social proof tools, aligning with social norms, fostering social communities, and monitoring and adapting your strategies, you can effectively harness the influence of social proof to build credibility, trust, and engagement with your target audience. With thoughtful execution and a deep understanding of human behavior, social proof becomes a potent tool for driving conversions, building brand loyalty, and shaping perceptions in today's interconnected digital landscape.

10.2 Influencing Through Authority

Influence through authority is a persuasive strategy that leverages the perception of expertise, credibility, and status to sway opinions, shape behavior, and drive decision-making. By positioning oneself or one's message as coming from a credible source or authoritative figure, individuals can effectively influence others and garner trust and respect. In this section, we will explore strategies for influencing through authority:

1. Establish Credibility and Expertise

Establish credibility and expertise in your field or domain by showcasing your knowledge, skills, and achievements. Position yourself as a trusted authority by sharing valuable insights, research findings, or industry expertise through content creation, public speaking engagements, or thought leadership initiatives. Demonstrate a deep understanding of relevant topics and trends to build trust and confidence among your audience.

2. Leverage Social Proof

Leverage social proof to reinforce your authority and credibility. Showcase endorsements, testimonials, or recommendations from respected individuals or organizations within your industry or niche. Highlight any affiliations, certifications, or credentials that validate your expertise and authority. By aligning yourself with established authorities, you can enhance your perceived credibility and influence.

3. Communicate with Confidence and Clarity

Communicate with confidence and clarity to convey authority and command attention. Use assertive language, tone, and body language to exude confidence and conviction in your message. Present your ideas or recommendations with clarity and precision, providing evidence or rationale to support your assertions. By projecting confidence and clarity, you inspire trust and respect in your audience.

4. Provide Value-Driven Insights

Provide value-driven insights and perspectives that demonstrate your authority and expertise. Offer practical advice, actionable tips, or thought-provoking analysis that addresses the needs and interests of your audience. Share unique or innovative solutions to common challenges or problems, positioning yourself as a knowledgeable resource and authority figure in your field.

5. Build Relationships and Networks

Build relationships and networks with other authorities or influencers within your industry or community. Collaborate on projects, contribute to discussions or forums, and participate in networking events or conferences to expand your reach and credibility. By associating yourself with other respected authorities, you can enhance your authority and influence through association.

6. Demonstrate Integrity and Authenticity

Demonstrate integrity and authenticity in all your interactions and communications. Uphold ethical standards and values that align with your authority positioning, avoiding misleading or manipulative tactics. Be transparent about your motives, intentions, and biases, and maintain consistency in your messaging and actions. By embodying integrity and authenticity, you reinforce your authority and trustworthiness.

7. Engage in Thought Leadership

Engage in thought leadership activities to establish yourself as a leading authority in your field. Publish articles, blogs, or whitepapers that contribute valuable insights or perspectives to relevant discussions or debates. Speak at industry events, participate in panel discussions, or host webinars to share your expertise and thought leadership with a broader audience. By actively contributing to thought leadership initiatives, you solidify your authority and influence within your industry.

Influencing through authority involves leveraging expertise, credibility, and status to persuade and inspire others. By establishing credibility and expertise, leveraging social proof, communicating with confidence and clarity, providing value-driven insights, building relationships and networks, demonstrating integrity and authenticity, and engaging in thought leadership, individuals can effectively wield authority to shape opinions, drive action, and make a positive impact in their respective fields. With strategic positioning and genuine leadership, authority becomes a powerful tool for driving change, fostering innovation, and inspiring others to achieve greatness.

10.3 Utilizing the Principle of Scarcity

The principle of scarcity is a psychological phenomenon that suggests people value items or opportunities more when they are perceived to be scarce or limited in availability. By leveraging scarcity effectively, individuals can influence behavior, drive demand, and create a sense of urgency or exclusivity. In this section, we will explore strategies for utilizing the principle of scarcity:

1. Create Limited-Time Offers

Create limited-time offers or promotions to capitalize on the principle of scarcity. Set deadlines or expiration dates for special discounts, sales, or promotions to create a sense of urgency and encourage immediate action. Highlight the limited availability of the offer to motivate customers to purchase before it's too late. By creating a sense of scarcity, you can stimulate demand and drive sales.

2. Offer Exclusive or Limited-Quantity Products

Offer exclusive or limited-quantity products to appeal to customers' desire for rarity and exclusivity. Create special editions, limited-run releases, or one-of-a-kind items that are only available for a limited time or in limited quantities. Highlight the unique features or benefits of these products to make them even more desirable. By offering scarce products, you can attract attention, generate buzz, and increase perceived value.

3. Implement Waiting Lists or Pre-Orders

Implement waiting lists or pre-orders for high-demand products or services to leverage the principle of scarcity. Allow customers to sign up in advance to secure their spot or reserve their item before it's officially released or restocked. Highlight the limited availability of spots or units to create anticipation and FOMO (fear of missing out) among potential customers. By tapping into people's desire to be part of an exclusive group, you can drive interest and demand.

4. Showcase Low Stock Levels

Showcase low stock levels or inventory scarcity to create a sense of urgency and scarcity. Display notifications or alerts indicating when a product is running low in stock or when there are only a few units left. Use phrases like "limited stock available" or "selling out fast" to communicate scarcity and prompt immediate action. By signaling scarcity, you can motivate customers to purchase before the item is gone.

5. Highlight Limited-Time Opportunities

Highlight limited-time opportunities or events to leverage the principle of scarcity. Promote exclusive events, workshops, or experiences that are only available for a short period or to a select group of participants. Emphasize the unique value or benefits of attending or participating in these events to create a sense of exclusivity and desirability. By offering limited-time opportunities, you can attract attention, drive engagement, and foster loyalty.

6. Use Social Proof to Amplify Scarcity

Use social proof to amplify the perception of scarcity and increase its impact. Showcase testimonials, reviews, or user-generated content that highlights the popularity or demand for your products or services. Display social proof notifications indicating when others have purchased or engaged with your offerings recently. By demonstrating social validation and endorsement, you can reinforce the scarcity effect and encourage action.

7. Maintain Authenticity and Transparency

Maintain authenticity and transparency when leveraging the principle of scarcity to avoid alienating or misleading customers. Be honest about the reasons for scarcity, whether it's due to limited production capacity, seasonal availability, or other factors. Avoid artificially creating scarcity or manipulating customers with deceptive tactics. By being genuine and transparent, you build trust and credibility with your audience.

Utilizing the principle of scarcity involves creating a sense of limited availability or exclusivity to influence behavior and drive action. By creating limited-time offers, offering exclusive or limited-quantity products, implementing waiting lists or pre-orders, showcasing low stock levels, highlighting limited-time opportunities, using social proof to amplify scarcity, and maintaining authenticity and transparency, individuals can effectively leverage scarcity to stimulate demand, drive sales, and create memorable experiences for customers. With strategic implementation and ethical considerations, scarcity becomes a powerful tool for driving engagement, fostering loyalty, and maximizing impact in today's competitive marketplace.

Chapter 11: Mastering Influence in the Digital Age

In today's interconnected world, mastering influence in the digital age requires a deep understanding of online platforms, communication channels, and social dynamics. The rise of social media, digital marketing, and online communities has transformed the landscape of influence, presenting new opportunities and challenges for individuals and organizations alike. In this chapter, we will explore strategies for mastering influence in the digital age:

Understanding the Digital Influence Ecosystem

1. Explore the Power of Social Media

Examine the role of social media platforms in shaping opinions, driving engagement, and amplifying influence. Discuss the unique features and functionalities of popular social media channels, such as Facebook, Instagram, Twitter, LinkedIn, and TikTok, and how they can be leveraged to reach and connect with diverse audiences.

2. Embrace Content Marketing Strategies

Embrace content marketing strategies to create valuable, relevant, and engaging content that resonates with your target audience. Explore different content formats, such as blog posts, videos, podcasts, infographics, and webinars, and leverage storytelling techniques to captivate and inspire your audience. Discuss the importance of consistency, authenticity, and audience-centricity in content creation.

Leveraging Digital Tools and Technologies

1. Harness Data Analytics and Insights

Harness data analytics and insights to understand audience behavior, preferences, and trends. Explore tools and technologies for tracking website traffic, social media engagement, and campaign performance, and use data-driven insights to optimize your strategies and tactics. Discuss the ethical considerations of data collection and privacy protection in the digital age.

2. Embrace Marketing Automation

Embrace marketing automation tools and platforms to streamline processes, personalize communication, and scale your influence efforts. Explore the capabilities of email marketing automation, customer relationship management (CRM) systems, and social media management tools for automating repetitive tasks, segmenting audiences, and delivering targeted messages.

Navigating Digital Communities and Networks

1. Engage in Online Communities

Engage in online communities and forums relevant to your niche or industry to build relationships, share insights, and establish authority. Participate in discussions, answer questions, and provide value to community members to position yourself as a trusted resource and influencer. Discuss strategies for fostering genuine connections and adding value in digital communities.

2. Cultivate Influential Relationships

Cultivate influential relationships with key stakeholders, industry influencers, and thought leaders in your field. Collaborate on joint ventures, co-create content, or participate in cross-promotional activities to expand your reach and credibility. Explore platforms for influencer marketing and partnership opportunities that align with your brand values and objectives.

Ethical Considerations in Digital Influence

1. Uphold Transparency and Authenticity

Uphold transparency and authenticity in all your digital influence efforts to build trust and credibility with your audience. Disclose sponsored content, affiliate partnerships, or conflicts of interest to maintain transparency and integrity. Avoid deceptive practices, such as buying followers or inflating engagement metrics that undermine trust and credibility.

2. Foster Positive Digital Citizenship

Foster positive digital citizenship by promoting responsible and ethical behavior online. Encourage respectful communication, constructive dialogue, and critical thinking in digital communities and networks. Advocate for digital literacy and media literacy to empower individuals to navigate the digital landscape responsibly and discern fact from fiction.

Mastering influence in the digital age requires a strategic and ethical approach to leveraging online platforms, digital tools, and virtual communities. By understanding the digital influence ecosystem, leveraging digital tools and technologies, navigating digital communities and networks, and upholding transparency and authenticity, individuals can effectively wield influence in today's interconnected world. With a commitment to ethical principles, continuous learning, and meaningful engagement, influence becomes a powerful force for driving positive change, fostering connections, and shaping a better digital future for all.

11.1 Influence Strategies in the Age of Social Media

In the age of social media, influence strategies have evolved to leverage the power of online platforms, communication channels, and social networks. With billions of users active on various social media platforms daily, mastering influence in this digital landscape requires a nuanced understanding of social dynamics, content creation, and audience engagement. In this section, we will explore effective influence strategies tailored to the age of social media:

1. Building Authentic Relationships

Focus on building authentic relationships with your audience by engaging in genuine interactions, providing valuable content, and fostering a sense of community. Actively respond to comments, messages, and mentions, and show appreciation for your followers' support and feedback. By cultivating trust and rapport with your audience, you establish a solid foundation for influence and credibility.

2. Creating Compelling Content

Create compelling and shareable content that resonates with your target audience and aligns with your brand identity and values. Experiment with different content formats, such as videos, images, infographics, and stories, to capture attention and spark engagement. Incorporate storytelling techniques, humor, and visual elements to make your content memorable and impactful.

3. Leveraging Influencer Partnerships

Collaborate with influencers and content creators in your niche or industry to amplify your reach and credibility. Identify influencers whose values and audience align with your brand, and explore partnership opportunities, such as sponsored content, product collaborations, or joint campaigns. Leveraging influencer partnerships can help you tap into new audiences and build social proof and validation.

4. Engaging in Conversations

Engage in conversations and participate in relevant discussions within your industry or community to demonstrate your expertise and thought leadership. Join industry-specific groups, forums, or Twitter chats to share insights, answer questions, and exchange ideas with peers and followers. By actively contributing to conversations, you position yourself as a knowledgeable and respected authority in your field.

5. Harnessing User-Generated Content

Harness user-generated content by encouraging your audience to create and share content related to your brand or products. Encourage user reviews, testimonials, or user-generated images and videos, and reshare them on your social media channels to showcase social proof and authenticity. By empowering your audience to become brand advocates, you amplify your reach and credibility.

6. Implementing Influencer Marketing

Implement influencer marketing campaigns to leverage the influence and reach of popular social media personalities. Identify influencers whose audience demographics align with your target market, and collaborate with them to promote your products or services authentically. Ensure that influencer partnerships are transparent, and the content aligns with your brand values and messaging.

7. Monitoring Trends and Insights

Monitor social media trends, conversations, and audience insights to stay informed about emerging topics, interests, and preferences. Use social listening tools and analytics platforms to track mentions, sentiment, and engagement metrics related to your brand or industry. By staying attuned to trends and insights, you can tailor your content and influence strategies to resonate with your audience effectively.

Influence strategies in the age of social media require a strategic and multifaceted approach that prioritizes authenticity, engagement, and relevance. By building authentic relationships, creating compelling content, leveraging influencer partnerships, engaging in conversations, harnessing user-generated content, implementing influencer marketing, and monitoring trends and insights, individuals and brands can effectively wield influence and drive meaningful connections in today's digital landscape. With a focus on building trust, fostering engagement, and adding value to the online community, influence becomes a powerful force for driving positive change and fostering brand loyalty in the age of social media.

11.2 Building Online Presence and Credibility

In the digital age, building a strong online presence and credibility is essential for individuals and brands looking to wield influence and engage with their target audience effectively. A robust online presence not only increases visibility but also fosters trust, credibility, and authority in the eyes of your audience. In this section, we will explore strategies for building a compelling online presence and establishing credibility:

1. Define Your Brand Identity

Start by defining your brand identity, including your values, mission, and unique selling proposition (USP). Clarify your target audience and understand their needs, preferences, and pain points. Develop a cohesive brand persona and visual identity that reflects your brand's personality and resonates with your audience.

2. Create High-Quality Content

Create high-quality and valuable content that educates, entertains, or inspires your audience. Tailor your content to address the interests, challenges, and aspirations of your target audience. Experiment with different content formats, such as blog posts, videos, podcasts, infographics, and social media posts, to engage with diverse audiences across various platforms.

3. Optimize Your Website and Social Profiles

Optimize your website and social media profiles to enhance visibility and credibility. Ensure that your website is user-friendly, mobile-responsive, and optimized for search engines (SEO). Use consistent branding, messaging, and imagery across all your digital channels to reinforce your brand identity and credibility.

4. Engage with Your Audience

Engage with your audience regularly through active participation in conversations, responding to comments and messages, and soliciting feedback. Foster genuine connections and relationships with your followers by showing authenticity, empathy, and transparency. Actively listen to your audience's needs and preferences and tailor your content and offerings accordingly.

5. Leverage Social Proof and Testimonials

Leverage social proof and testimonials to build credibility and trust with your audience. Showcase positive reviews, testimonials, endorsements, and social media mentions to demonstrate the value and impact of your products or services. Encourage satisfied customers to share their experiences and recommendations publicly to amplify social proof.

6. Demonstrate Expertise and Authority

Demonstrate your expertise and authority in your niche or industry by sharing valuable insights, knowledge, and thought leadership content. Write blog posts, articles, or whitepapers that showcase your expertise and provide solutions to common problems or challenges faced by your audience. Speak at industry events, participate in webinars, or host workshops to position yourself as a trusted authority.

7. Collaborate with Influencers and Partners

Collaborate with influencers, industry experts, and strategic partners to expand your reach and credibility. Identify individuals or organizations whose values and audience align with yours and explore partnership opportunities, such as guest blogging, co-hosting events, or cross-promotional campaigns. Collaborative efforts can help you tap into new audiences and enhance your credibility through association.

Building a strong online presence and credibility requires a strategic and holistic approach that encompasses branding, content creation, engagement, social proof, expertise, and collaboration. By defining your brand identity, creating high-quality content, optimizing your digital channels, engaging with your audience, leveraging social proof, demonstrating expertise, and collaborating with influencers and partners, you can establish a compelling online presence and earn the trust and loyalty of your audience. With consistency, authenticity, and a commitment to adding value, you can position yourself or your brand as a credible and influential force in the digital landscape.

11.3 Avoiding Common Pitfalls in Digital Influence

While digital influence offers tremendous opportunities for individuals and brands to connect with their audience and drive impact, it also presents certain risks and challenges. In the pursuit of influence, it's crucial to navigate the digital landscape with caution and integrity to avoid common pitfalls that could undermine credibility and trust. In this section, we will explore some of the most prevalent pitfalls of digital influence and strategies for avoiding them:

1. Lack of Authenticity

One of the most significant pitfalls of digital influence is the lack of authenticity. Authenticity is the foundation of trust and credibility in the online space. Avoid presenting a false or exaggerated image of yourself or your brand, as it can lead to skepticism and alienation from your audience. Instead, strive to be genuine, transparent, and true to your values and identity.

2. Over-Promotion

Another common pitfall is over-promotion, where individuals or brands prioritize self-promotion over providing value to their audience. Constantly bombarding your audience with promotional messages can come across as spammy and insincere, leading to disengagement and loss of trust. Strike a balance between promotion and value-driven content to maintain audience interest and engagement.

3. Neglecting Engagement

Neglecting engagement with your audience is another pitfall that can hinder your digital influence efforts. Building meaningful connections and relationships with your audience requires active engagement and interaction. Respond to comments, messages, and mentions promptly, and foster dialogue and discussion around your content and offerings. By neglecting engagement, you risk appearing distant and disconnected from your audience.

4. Ignoring Negative Feedback

Ignoring negative feedback or criticism is a common pitfall that can damage your reputation and credibility. Instead of dismissing or deleting negative comments or reviews, address them constructively and professionally. Use criticism as an opportunity for learning and improvement, and demonstrate your commitment to listening and responding to your audience's concerns.

5. Misuse of Influencer Marketing

Misuse of influencer marketing is another pitfall that can backfire on brands. Partnering with influencers solely based on their follower count or reach, without considering their relevance, authenticity, or alignment with your brand values, can result in ineffective or even damaging collaborations. Take the time to vet influencers carefully and ensure that their audience demographics and values align with yours.

6. Lack of Transparency

Lack of transparency in digital influence can erode trust and credibility with your audience. Disclose sponsored content, affiliate partnerships, or other commercial relationships transparently to maintain integrity and authenticity. Be upfront about any incentives or compensation received for promoting products or services, and avoid misleading or deceptive practices that could compromise trust.

7. Failure to Adapt

Failure to adapt to changing trends, algorithms, and audience preferences is another pitfall that can hinder your digital influence efforts. Stay agile and responsive to shifts in the digital landscape, and continuously experiment with new strategies, tactics, and platforms. Keep abreast of emerging trends and technologies, and be willing to evolve and adapt your approach accordingly.

Avoiding common pitfalls in digital influence requires a proactive approach that prioritizes authenticity, engagement, transparency, and adaptability. By staying true to your values, providing value to your audience, actively engaging with your community, addressing criticism constructively, vetting influencers carefully, maintaining transparency, and remaining adaptable to change, you can navigate the digital landscape with integrity and effectiveness. With a focus on building trust and credibility, you can cultivate a loyal and engaged audience and achieve a meaningful impact in the digital age.

Conclusion:

In the journey through the pages of "Power of Influence: Master the Art of Persuasion with Proven Strategies and Techniques to Communicate Effectively, Influence Others, and Achieve Success," we've delved deep into the intricacies of human psychology, communication, and persuasion. We've explored the timeless principles and practical techniques that empower individuals to wield influence with integrity, empathy, and effectiveness.

From understanding the dynamics of influence to mastering persuasion strategies, navigating ethical considerations, and overcoming resistance, this book has equipped you with the knowledge and tools needed to become a master influencer in every aspect of your life.

Throughout these chapters, you've learned to harness the principles of persuasion, leverage cognitive biases, and tap into emotional intelligence to connect with others on a deeper level. You've discovered the importance of building rapport, fostering trust, and tailoring your communication to different audiences. You've explored the nuances of influence in professional settings, personal relationships, and the digital age, uncovering strategies for success in every context.

As you embark on your journey to apply these insights and techniques in your own life, remember that true influence is not about manipulation or coercion but about empowerment and transformation. It's about inspiring others to see the world from a new perspective, to embrace change, and to achieve their fullest potential.

Whether you aspire to lead teams, build strong relationships, or make a positive impact in your community, the power of influence lies within you. By honing your communication skills, cultivating empathy, and embodying authenticity, you can shape hearts and minds, drive change, and create a better world for yourself and those around you.

So go forth with confidence, knowing that you possess the knowledge, skills, and wisdom to wield influence with purpose and integrity. As you apply the lessons learned in this book, may you unlock your full potential as a master influencer and achieve success in all your endeavors.

Embrace the power of influence, and let your journey toward greater impact and fulfillment begin.